To Roy —
with best wishes for
continued success —

Sincerely,

Earl V. Bittman
Les Wilber

5/9/84

6-1-84

PRINCIPLES AND VALUES
FOR
COLLEGE AND UNIVERSITY
ADMINISTRATION

Wolf in the woods setting up a plow.
Grasshopper looking on telling him how.

(From an ancient fable)

PRINCIPLES AND VALUES FOR COLLEGE AND UNIVERSITY ADMINISTRATION

Toward the Improvement of the Learning Environment

by

EARL V. PULLIAS
Professor Emeritus of Higher Education
University of Southern California
Member of the Los Angeles County
Board of Education

and

LESLIE WILBUR
Professor of Higher Education
Chairman of the Department
University of Southern California
One-time Chairman of the U.S.C.
Faculty Senate

Philosophical Library
New York

Library of Congress Cataloging in Publication Data

Pullias, Earl Vivon, 1907-
    Principles and values for college and university administration.

    Bibliography: p. 89
    Includes index.
    1. Universities and colleges—United States—Adminis-
tration. I. Wilbur, Leslie. II. Title.
LB2341.P85   1984   378.73   84-4259
ISBN 0-8022-2443-1

This book is dedicated to our wives,
Pauline Boyce Pullias and Norma Lash Wilbur:
friends, critics and partners in all our endeavors,
not least the writing of this book.

TABLE OF CONTENTS

Acknowledgments xi

Part I

      Introduction and Background 3
1. Nature and Purpose of the Book 3
2. The Application of Principle to Behavior 4
3. A Chief Concern: the Steady Improvement
    of the Environment of Learning 5

Part II

      Some Basic Principles of College and
      University Administration 11
1. Purposes of the Institution 11
2. Decisions Planned 12
3. Decisions in Process 13
4. Decisions Reached and Announced 14
5. Response to Problem Situations 15
6. Responsibility and Competence 15
7. Delegation of Duty and Authority 16
8. Courtesy and Human Relations 17
9. Gross Violation of Acceptable Behavior Standards ... 18
10. Dealing with Grievances 19

11. Contentious Complaints 20
12. Recognition of Staff and Faculty Achievement 21
13. Favoritism 22
14. The Responsibility and Role of College and
    University Faculty Members 23
15. Freedom......................................24
16. Change and Stability 26
17. Attitudes toward Youth.........................27
18. Students and Academic Governance 29
19. Diversity and Variety in Thought
    and Behavior 31
20. Economy 32
21. Financial Accountability 33
22. Responsible Speech and Writing 34
23. Mistakes......................................36
24. Institutional Tradition and Practice...............37
25. Campus Guests 39
26. Gossip and Pressure 40
27. The Danger of Crowd Psychology 41
28. Foresight or Prometheus 42
29. Power of the Administrative Office 43
30. Pacing Activity 44
31. Decisiveness...................................45
32. Successful Striving and Morale 46
33. Faculty and Staff Discussion 47
34. Trusted Counselors of the Administrator 49
35. The Administrative Office and the Person
    Who Temporarily Occupies the Office.............50
36. Relations with the Lay Board 51

Part III

    Theoretical Considerations: Background
    for Principles..................................57
    Introduction 57
1. The Higher Learning: Teaching and Research
   in College and University.......................59
2. Higher Education in Modern Society 62

3. The Governance of Higher Education:
   Some Basic Principles 66
4. A Neglected Dimension of Educational
   Leadership: the Leader as a Person 74
5. Academic Governance: Some Misunderstandings 83

Part IV

   Selected References 89

Part V

   A Note on the Training and Experience
   of the Authors.................................95

Index...101

ACKNOWLEDGMENTS

Much of what we would ordinarily wish to say under "acknowledgments" has been said in a somewhat different way and in more detail in Part V of this book. In giving a relatively full account of our background, including training and experience, we have indicated some of the debts we owe to people and institutions who have helped us to write this book.

Beyond what is said in the introduction and in Part V, certain other formal acknowledgments should be made. We owe much, in a sense most, to the large number of high-quality graduate students who have studied with us. We have discussed all these ideas with them, and wish very much they could read and react again to these thoughts before the manuscript goes to press. They have been valuable teachers and constructive critics for us.

Also, we owe much to faculty members who have worked with us here at U.S.C., at the colleges where we tried to practice good administration, and at institutions where we have counseled and advised over the years. The open, thoughtful, and sometimes painfully frank academic community is a great teacher. We appreciate all we have learned from our colleagues, and wish we had listened better and learned more.

It is almost superfluous to say that we could not have done either the background or the direct work on this book without the constant help, candid reactions, unswerving loyalty, interest and encouragement of our wives, to whom the book is dedicated.

We deeply appreciate the indispensable work Bess Davis Owens has done as a skilled typist in getting the manuscript ready for publication.

Grateful acknowledgment is made to the following publishers, agents and other copyright holders for permission to reprint materials previously published:

Society for the Advancement of Education, Inc. for three articles by Earl V. Pullias: "Ten Principles of College Administration" in *School and Society*, Feb. 1972; "College and University Administration: Ten More Principles" in *Intellect*, April 1973; and "College and University Administration: Ten Additional Principles" in *Intellect*, Nov. 1973. Used by Permission of Society for the Advancement of Education, Inc.

William C. Brown Company for "Higher Education in Modern Society" from *Toward Excellence in College Teaching*, 1963, by Earl V. Pullias and Aileen Lockhart. Used by permission from William C. Brown Company.

Educational Research Quarterly for "The Higher Learning: Teaching and Research in College and University," Fall 1978. Used by permission by Educational Research Quarterly.

PART I

Introduction and Background

The validity and practical value of a book on college and university administration depend in great measure on the nature and purpose of the volume and the credentials of the authors, especially their training and experience. Parts I and V are planned to give the reader that background information, and thus to put the remainder of the book in meaningful context.

1. *Nature and purpose of the book.* There is a large literature on administration in general, particularly as it relates to government, business, the military and other large public and private organizations. There is a growing body of research and theory which under takes to apply the general principles of administration to the special conditions of colleges and universities, although it can be said that still the literature on college and university administration is relatively thin. The authors are reasonably well acquainted with research and theory on administration in general, and on college and university administration in particular. The basic purpose of this book does not seem to warrant detailed references and footnoting.

The majority of these principles were originally published in a series of three journal articles and were very well received, although the audience was inevitably limited. There have been many requests to bring these ideas together to make them available in permanent form. There has been some rewriting of the original statements, some reorganization, and additional principles not previously published have been added for this volume.

The background principles dealing with the nature and purposes of the higher learning make up Part III of the book. These statements are, of course, in no sense definitive or exhaustive, but they are intended to emphasize the importance of this area of study for college and university administration. We hope these ideas, which we believe are basically sound historically and theoretically, stimulate thought and discussion on college and university campuses. If these sections raise some of the basic issues about the nature and purposes of the higher learning they will have served a good purpose.

No attempt has been made to designate authorship of the various parts of the book. The authors have worked so closely and in such harmony that the ideas are mutually held, although of course they differ on some points. A word about the original plan for the book and why the present approach was adopted will illustrate this point.

The original plan was to make the volume a dialogue between a faculty member and a president on some major practical problems of college and university administration, with Dr. Pullias presenting the faculty view and Dr. Wilbur, because of his experience as a college president, giving the reaction of the chief administrator. As the principles now comprising Part II developed, it became clear that in the case of these two authors the understandings and emphasis were so much the same that a dialogue in the usual sense would not be possible or useful. The decision was then reached to present the principles as they now appear, knowing that in many situations they will naturally stimulate discussion or dialogue.

2. *The Application of Principle to Behavior.* Our long experience causes us to know how difficult it is in practical affairs to apply or practice even the simplest and evidently sound principle. Our hope is that to have some useful principles vividly and steadily before an academic community, and especially before those with administrative responsibility and before the general faculty, may help to prevent the neglect of practices which are not really difficult to apply. If a cooperative attitude—one of general concern for the welfare of the institution and all who are a part of it—can be developed and maintained, each part of the organization can help the other parts to strive

to apply the best principles they know. Such an attitude is, of course, hard to achieve in an organization, and it will exist only in degree, but by conscious and persistent effort, progress can be made toward a spirit of mutual helpfulness.

The hypothesis of this book is that there is a body of principles which can be known and stated, and if used in administration would greatly improve the effectiveness of the work of colleges and universities. We believe that administrative behavior should be guided by principle rather than being approached in terms of expediency or immediate emergency demands. It is our hope that this book may contribute to progress toward administration by principle as opposed to personal desire or the apparent pressures of the time. Such progress depends first of all upon the recognition that the principles arise from the nature, purposes and proper processes of the higher learning. They should be applied with understanding and appreciation of that fundamental relationship. Thoughtful application is a large requirement and in actual situations will rarely be achieved and often only gradually approached: A hope for perfection quickly or easily achieved is a great enemy to genuine progress.

3. *A Chief Concern: the Steady Improvement of the Environment of Learning.* The higher learning, whether at a community college, a small liberal arts college, or a large, complex, research-centered university, does a very special work that in fact no other institution can do. This work involves two closely interrelated processes: (1) the imaginative transmission of old knowledge through what is broadly called teaching, and (2) the constant search for new knowledge which is added to and integrated with the old knowledge and thus enriches the process of education.

It is the nature of the college or university that these two tasks must be so interrelated and intertwined that they are a basic part of each other. Surely teaching can and does take place in a variety of places and circumstances—the home, the church or temple, on the job—but the fact that teaching does take place somewhere does not make that place the higher learning, a college or a university. In like manner, the search for new truth may be found in numerous places and circumstances—in fact, the search for truth, both the discovery of the new which is rare and the discovery or rediscovery of old knowledge, is very nearly the nature of human life. The search may be carried on by a person alone, by a technical institution, or by a business, but this search for new truth, however diligent or effective, is not as such the higher learning. Intellectual inquiry as an organized community effort, among the four or five most significant discoveries of the human mind, is a delicate, difficult-to-describe combination of teaching the old and discovering the new, carried on under very special circumstances and conditions.

The process of the higher learning requires for its optimum effectiveness an organized community of a very special kind. This community must have buildings and grounds, a considerable nonprofessional, or at least semiprofessional, staff (from caretakers of grounds to chief administrative officers), a complex budget and, above all, a selected corps of highly trained faculty who are teachers and researchers, and students who are principally learners, who have completed the phases of elementary and secondary learning and are thus prepared as candidates for the community of scholars. There are libraries, laboratories, museums, playing fields, living quarters, eating places, chapels, observatories—all the means for carrying on most effectively the teaching and discovery process in a very special atmosphere and spirit.

Evidently such a community can and usually does become very complex and thus must be administered. The key point in this connection is that all of this administrative activity should contribute to the production and maintenance of the best possible conditions or environment for carrying on the process of the higher learning. A minimum requirement is that no administrative behavior should threaten or damage the quality of that environment. The central emphasis of this book is that the conscientious and persistent application of a few relatively simple, almost common sense principles would do much to help college and university administrations meet that standard. Thus, every principle presented in this book and every practice implied should meet the crucial criterion: Would the application of this principle improve the environment so essential to the effective functioning of the higher learning?

One final word about the learning environment which may help to drive home the basic significance of this point. The evidence is strong, we believe overwhelming, that the general, overall atmosphere of a college or university as a whole community educates and promotes the genuine search for new truth more profoundly and more permanently than any of its separate parts or processes. As former English majors, we are partial to a poetic term to describe best this atmosphere, namely "spirit of place," a result of the presence and proper working together of all the parts that make up the community of scholars, a *gestalt*, that is much more and much more powerful than the segmented parts.

Good administration consciously seeks to create and maintain the optimum spirit of place or environment or atmosphere for the higher learning.

PART II

Some Basic Principles of College and University Administration

Here are thirty-six common-sense principles of administration stated briefly and illustrated chiefly from the teacher's point of view:

Principle 1   Purposes of the Institution

STATE THE PURPOSES AND IDEALS OF THE COLLEGE OR UNIVERSITY CLEARLY, CONVINCINGLY, AND OFTEN TO ALL CONSTITUENCIES OF THE INSTITUTION: FACULTY, STUDENTS, BOARD, ALUMNI, STAFF, PATRONS, AND THE VARIOUS PUBLICS THE INSTITUTION SERVES.

The Administrator Is the Chief Voice for the Institution: Its Purposes, Processes, and Goals Must Not Be Taken for Granted, but Must Be Stated Again and Again.

The purposes and the major processes of the institution should be kept before all segments of the academic community—board, students, faculty, patrons, staff, and the various publics of the college or university. Probably the most ominous threat to the quality of modern life is the loss of large purposes which are basic to direction and meaning. Colleges and universities are no exception—without inspiring and informative leadership, they rapidly become the most divided and confused of all our institutions.

11

A certain cynicism and accompanying fear have become almost endemic in institutions of higher learning. Few administators seem to be clear about the large purposes of higher learning in general, or of their specific institutions in particular. Those who may have a reasonably clear vision of purpose often seem unable to state the purpose with force and conviction. The result is that many institutions drift or flounder. Each segment—faculty, students, etc.—failing to be engaged in large purposes of the institution as a whole, by the very nature of human life rapidly develops small, individual, and often petty purposes. Each fragment of the institution pursuing its own small goals produces division, cross purpose, and even confusion.

A major task of the administrator is to state and continually to restate, wisely and skillfully, the purposes of the institution: to help every individual who is in any way a part of the institution to understand and to feel its major purposes and to be inspired by his or her part in realizing those purposes. All great college administrators have manifested this skill. Perhaps William Rainey Harper, first president of the University of Chicago, was one of the most skillful in applying this principle.

This principle in no sense implies a static, fixed institution. Emphasis should be placed on the fact that a good institution of higher learning is dynamic and hence constantly changing. Although large general purposes arise from the nature of the higher learning and remain quite constant, specific sub-purposes and the means of achieving them need constant review and study by the institutions.

Principle 2   Decisions Planned

INFORM EARLY AND AS NEARLY AS POSSIBLE ALL INDIVIDUALS WHO ARE OR WILL BE AFFECTED BY THE DECISION.

Decisions Appearing as Surprises Undermine Confidence and Destroy Team Spirit.

In any decision-making process, those who will be affected by the decision should be informed and, if possible, consulted. Even in such simple matters as physical changes in buildings or grounds, informing and consulting students and faculty and, in certain cases, alumni can be of great value to morale.

The goal is to help all who are involved in the institution to feel that the institution's business is basically their business. The application of this principle does not mean that decisions are bogged down in endless committees or fruitless discussion. In most cases, careful, authentic, and consistent information will do the job. No individual likes to feel that things which profoundly affect his or her interest and welfare are taking place without his or her knowledge. The idea is that simple.

Principle 3   Decisions in Process

LET ALL WHO ARE INVOLVED IN MAKING THE DECISION KNOW THE LIMITS OF THEIR INFLUENCE OR POWER IN MAKING THE FINAL DECISION.

For an Individual or a Particular Group To Misconceive Their Part in Making the Final Decision Is Demoralizing: Most Important Decisions in an Academic Community Involve Many Levels of Organization and Many Individuals.

The people who are consulted when a decision is being sought (faculty, students, alumni, etc.) should be helped to understand the way in which their advice or counsel will be used. A failure to understand how the decision process works, who is involved, and who makes the final decision is a source of much misunderstanding.

Whatever is done, some contentious and self-centered persons may feel that their judgment should have prevailed, but, in a reasonably healthy community, these individuals are relatively few. If given the proper information, most persons will accept the fact that they, or the committee of which they are working members, are a part of a complex and sometimes long process. Understanding is the key here. The individual or the committee should understand as clearly as possible the limits and extent of its role and responsibility.

In cases where final authority is clear and can be meaningfully identified, a distinction should be made between an authority and an advisory role. As a rule, in academic process the two types of role overlap and are intermingled.

Principle 4 Decisions Reached and Announced

THE COMMUNITY OF SCHOLARS (THE COLLEGE OR UNIVERSITY: FACULTY, STUDENTS, STAFF, ETC.) SHOULD HEAR THE DECISION FIRST.

To Be the First To Hear About Important Decisions Does Much To Make One Feel an Important Part of the Organization: A Second- or Third-Rate Citizen Hears Important News Indirectly or Second-hand.

The faculty, the student body, and the staff—the campus community—should be the first to hear about important decisions and developments. Although they may have had adequate participation in the process, the nature and timing of the announcement of the final decision are important.

The faculty, staff, and students often get their information about a new president or other significant decisions from gossip, the public press, radio, or television. Thus, they come to feel as outsiders, alien to those who make the decisions—an atmosphere conducive to hostility and destructive dissension.

This principle is violated or neglected in all types and sizes of institutions. Perhaps the large institutions are worse offenders because of their unwieldy size, but there is not much difference in varied types of institutions: All are offenders. We are not referring here to participation in the decision-making process. A representative committee may have worked long and hard on the decision, but then fail to inform the group most affected by, and concerned with, the decision before it is announced publicly. The idea is simple, but of great psychological importance. The academic family should know about the family decisions first and should not have to hear them from other sources.

Members of the campus community often are asked by outsiders to comment upon or to explain decisions announced publicly. Aside from the embarrassment of ignorance, the uninformed faculty member is unlikely to defend or explain an administrative action that comes as a surprise. We are aware it is often difficult to communicate fully with faculty members. They may be negligent about reading their mail and may ignore campus newspapers and department bulletins. The creative administrator finds ways to surmount these barriers, and avoids being frustrated by them.

Principle 5 Response to Problem Situations

INDIVIDUALS NEAREST THE PROBLEM SHOULD DECIDE AND ACT FIRST.

The Individual Who Has Immediate Responsibility and Is on the Ground Should Be Expected and Allowed To Solve the Problem Whenever Possible.

As a general rule, the responsible person nearest to the involved situation should make the decision. Sometimes it is necessary to bring in more people and thus broaden the base, but, in most cases, the person nearest the problem should handle it.

An evident example of this point is the teacher in his or her classroom or laboratory. In making decisions, teachers must be sensitive to the needs and feelings of the larger community as expressed in general policy and custom, but they should be allowed, and even urged, to solve their own problems. So it should be with departments, various deans, and agencies. The farther the decision is from the persons immediately involved and concerned, the greater the likelihood of foolish mistakes and of harm being done to morale and confidence.

This requires that administrators and faculty foster and encourage individual responsibility and decisions. This problem is complicated by the fact that a climate of respect for peers and acceptance of personal responsibility is difficult to maintain in an adversarial climate.

Principle 6 Responsibility and Competence

RESPONSIBILITY SHOULD CORRESPOND CLEARLY TO COMPETENCE.

Care Should Be Taken that Responsibility Be Assigned Only to People Who Have and Are Known To Have Adequate Competence in That Area.

Consistent effort should be made to enable all in the college or university to understand the principle that there must be a relationship between responsibility and competence—that individuals can be given responsibility only in an area where they have established their competence. To put it another way, the boundaries of competence and responsibility should coincide.

There is a widespread tendency in an academic community for individuals to believe that their competence in a specialized area makes them worthy of responsibility in areas where they have little or no competence. For example, the professors often seem convinced that they could manage the budget better than the business manager, or buildings and grounds—particularly parking—better than the plant engineer.

This tendency to talk, and even to try to act, outside one's area of competence is quite human and, to a degree, valuable in a democratic society, but in an academic community, where special competence is so vital, it must be directed carefully. The effectiveness of any organization rests on respect for competence and the adjusting of responsibility to competence. The administrator should keep an eye out for competence, talent, and special skill, and should provide a use for them whenever possible.

A corollary of matching responsibility with competence is that of occasionally placing responsibility where there is potential rather than demonstrated competence. This kind of assignment is one which may accelerate growth in subordinates, but it also introduces the danger of failure which may injure the reputation of the president or other administrator as well as the person directly responsible.

This point relates to the administator as risk-taker, one who has the perception to estimate abilities which require opportunities to emerge, and who has the courage to provide opportunities which may, if mishandled, reflect on his own judgment.

Principle 7   Delegation of Duty and Authority

WHENEVER DUTY OR RESPONSIBILITY IS DELEGATED TAKE CARE TO DELEGATE AUTHORITY AT THE SAME TIME AND IN CORRESPONDING DEGREE.

If Responsibility Is Delegated and the Needed Authority and Means To Carry Out That Responsibility Are Withheld or Grudgingly Given, the Most Competent Person May Be Frustrated.

When responsibility is delegated—as it should and must be in any organization—corresponding authority should be delegated within reasonable limits. Few things are more destructive of morale than to give a person the responsibility for doing a task or for solving a problem and neglect to give, or at some point to withdraw, the authority needed to do the job.

Of course, in very sensitive areas, authority may have to be limited or, in rare cases, authority may have to be withdrawn, but, if done frequently, the delegation of responsibility becomes impossible and the administrator finds himself burdened with all responsibility—a highly destructive situation for the administrator and for the institution.

Unless a mistake threatens to be too costly—often a difficult decision to make in practice—it is usually better to suffer the consequences of the mistake than to undercut or reverse the decision of an individual or committee which had, or thought it had, authority to act.

Principle 8   Courtesy and Human Relations

NEVER DEVIATE FROM BEING COURTEOUS WHEN DEALING WITH PEOPLE.

To Be Discourteous, or To Appear To Be, to Any Member of the Academic Community Is a Serious and Often Costly Mistake: Academic People Have Very Sensitive Egos and Long Memories.

The practice of basic courtesy is essential in dealing with members of the academic community. Under the pressure of continuous work and complex and often conflicting demands, administrators tend to become irritable and fractious. College personnel, both faculty and students, are peculiarly sensitive—they have tender egos. They forget a slight or any affront very slowly, especially if it is given in public.

There is no suggestion here that the administrator be vacillating or be less than genuinely frank. Courtesy, which basically is an understanding of, and respect for, the other person's feelings and thought, is in harmony with forthrightness. Directly reprimanding a person, regardless of the nature of his or her mistake, involves a serious risk. There is a dangerous theory, frequently promoted in semipopular psychological writing, that severely reprimanding an adult—a faculty member or a college student—may clear the air and serve as a foundation for good relations. Our experience leads us to conclude that an adult rarely forgets or forgives such occasions. President Charles W. Eliot, who developed Harvard from a small college to a great university and is considered an all-time great in college administration, was especially wise in dealing with disturbing personal behavior and attitudes on the part of faculty.

Principle 9   Gross Violation of Acceptable Behavior Standards

CLEAR AND REPEATED GROSS BEHAVIOR INAPPROPRIATE TO THE ACADEMIC COMMUNITY MUST BE DEALT WITH PROMPTLY AND FIRMLY WITHIN DUE PROCESS.

Although the Community of Scholars Respects and Encourages Independence and Variety, It Has Standards Basic to Effective Functioning: The Violation of These Standards Requires Prompt and Firm Action.

A process for, and habit of, dealing swiftly and firmly with behavior which is clearly outside mutually established standards of the academic community is essential for administrators. They should be sensitively aware of the limits of their power, and should take care not to violate or shortcut due process. When due process clearly has been served, or the situation is so acute as to demand emergency measures, it is extremely dangerous for the chief administrative officer to hesitate or vacillate in taking necessary action.

A profound psychological principle is involved in this point. In the whole academic community, there are always many who do not behave in terms of deeply considered principle and who, therefore, may be swayed by the current wind—the *Zeitgeist*—particularly in highly emotional situations. Stated in another way, grossly undesirable behavior, ignored or neglected, tends to drive out acceptable or desirable behavior.

For example, if the gross behavior of the 1960s, which approached or reached verbal and physical violence so destructive of the academic spirit and community, had been dealt with swiftly and promptly in its very beginnings, higher learning might have been saved great misery and damage. Instead, many administrators seemed to lack the courage or wisdom to act decisively to support the deep conscience and concord of the academic community.

This principle applies only to gross behavior clearly in violation of the basic process of the college or university, and, of course, must not be used to violate proper freedom, to inhibit legitimate protest, or to protect injustice.

Principle 10 Dealing with Grievances

LET THE AGGRIEVED PERSON BE HEARD AS SOON AS POSSIBLE AND REASONABLY FULLY.

The Seriousness of an Offense or Grievance Is Determined Largely by How the Aggrieved Person Perceives the Offense: To Be Heard Promptly and Fully Often Does Much To Change the Perception.

Grievance procedure in the academic community should be available and clearly understood. If individuals consider themselves aggrieved, then, so far as they are concerned, they are aggrieved. In such cases, perception, even false perception, becomes reality.

In any sizable group there will be people who perceive themselves to be wronged when clearly they have not been. Some of these will be pathological or nearly so. These persons are a burden to themselves and to the institution, requiring special, sometimes very firm, treatment.

Our concern here is not with the pathological, but with the very human need to have a fair and sincere hearing of one's concern. Often, an individual's greatest needs are to be heard sympathetically and to know that he or she can be heard if the need arises.

In order to apply this principle well the administrator must learn to listen. Intelligent listening is much more than being silent while waiting to speak. Listening is both a communicative skill and a fundamental means of relating to other persons. Nevertheless it is remarkable how many administrators, and other faculty members, rely largely on their abilities in spoken and written communication. As a result of this reliance they may come to be poor listeners, especially in dealing with grievances. Careful listening can, however, be a significant therapeutic avenue for a faculty member, a student, or a board member who feels a need to be heard, to feel that the institution is aware of his or her problem, even though the awareness may not lead to an immediate or satisfactory response.

Principle 11   Contentious Complaints

DO NOT SPEND UNDUE OR DISPROPORTIONATE TIME AND ENERGY ON TRYING TO SATISFY CHRONIC COMPLAINERS: AVOID TOO MUCH EMPHASIS ON THE SQUEAKY WHEEL.

Every Individual in the Community of Scholars Should Be Respected, but Regular or Prompt Responses to Chronic Fussing or Complaining Can Establish Fussing and Complaining as the Best Way To Get Results.

The practice of responding chiefly to complaints—of being caught in the trap of "greasing the squeaky wheel" psychology—should be avoided as much as is practicable. There are persons on all college and university faculties who, since childhood, have tried to, and often succeeded in, getting what they wanted by causing trouble.

Of course, administrators rarely have the power to give a faculty member, student, or student organization precisely what is demanded. In cases where they do have the power, they should be careful about rewarding complaint. If administrators respond chiefly to complaints, it soon becomes known that the best way to get a condition improved is to raise a fuss, and gradually even those in the organization who would work through courteous process begin to use the method of noisy complaint.

This principle does not imply that a genuine concern of a member of the community of scholars should be ignored because it is expressed unattractively or even discourteously. There is a danger that the administrator will refuse to examine with care a situation that needs attention simply because the person who presents the problem is unpleasant or even somewhat irrational. Strange as it may seem, such people often have an uncanny ability to put their finger on things that do need attention.

Administrators seek to learn of conditions by every legitimate means, to consider the situation on its merits, and to respond to it through proper process. Thus, they try to improve undesirable conditions in ways that are equitable and which do not unduly reward contentious complaint.

Principle 12   Recognition of Staff and Faculty Achievement

SIGNIFICANT ACHIEVEMENT SHOULD BE APPRO-PRIATELY RECOGNIZED, TAKING CARE THAT THE RECOGNITION IS AND APPEARS TO BE SINCERE.

All People, but Especially Academic People, Hunger for Recognition from Those they Respect: Achievement in Any Organization, but Especially in Large Ones, Tends To Be Taken for Granted or Lost in the Shuffle; the Good Administrator Is Sensitive to Effective, Fine Performance and Develops a Sincere Personal Method of Giving Proper Recognition. This Principle Must Be Applied with Great Subtlety and Integrity or It Is Considered Phony and Backfires.

The administrator should take note of significant achievement by members of the academic community. A note or a personal word from an administrator (president, dean, department or division chairman) to a faculty or staff member, recognizing an article, speech, or other work that is especially well done is a stimulation and encouragement to most staff and faculty members. It is of utmost importance that this kind of recognition be given in sincere appreciation and with a minimum of patronizing or condescension.

Academic people are quite sensitive to pretense or phoniness of any kind, but like other people they hunger for appreciation from those whom they respect. In this connection, it is well for the administrator to remember that faculties in colleges and universities do not consider administrators as their superiors in the usual sense, but they tend to think of them as colleagues with special responsibility. The mere fact that administrators know something of what is being achieved and care enough to speak of the achievements adds much to the unity of the campus.

The best administrators will probably develop systematic means to keep informed, yet, as mentioned earlier, they will guard carefully against using, or appearing to use, recognition-giving as a gimmick in "human relations." The increasing size of most institutions makes the wise application of this principle difficult. Perhaps a plan by which announcements of the most noteworthy achievements were distributed systematically from departments to deans and to the president's office would be of practical help. The key, however, would seem to be a genuine interest in and respect for the work and special accomplishments of faculty and staff colleagues: Given this, the rest is likely to follow.

Principle 13   Favoritism

EQUITY AND WHAT IS CONCEIVED AS EQUITY OR FAIRNESS ARE BASIC TO GOOD MORALE IN THE COMMUNITY OF SCHOLARS.

The Administrator Who Has Special Favorites in the Organization or Seems To Have Made Favorites Cannot Long Retain the Respect of the Whole Academic Community.

Favoritism, or what appears to be favoritism, is especially harmful to morale. Of course, the administrators are human and they inevitably like some people better than others. Perhaps, in spite of their best efforts, they will show their likes or dislikes, but any favoritism, or the appearance of it, impairs general confidence.

There is always the danger that favoritism will express itself in special treatment which is, or appears to be, unfair. Careful adherence to equity, as a rule, is much more important for morale than is the actual amount of such items as salaries or travel budgets. Hardship may not be easy to bear under any circumstances, but most academic people will bear it well if the hardship is understood and if there is reasonable equity.

What seems to be favoritism may be a reflection of the administrator's uneven recognition of merit or individuality. Ideally, every faculty member's contribution, however modest, should receive occasional recognition. If such recognition is generally rare, those who receive it may be seen as favorites of the administrator. (See Principle 33.)

Principle 14   The Responsibility and Role of College and University Faculty Members

THE TEACHER IN AN INSTITUTION OF HIGHER LEARNING IS AN OFFICER OF THE CORPORATION OR ORGANIZED COMMUNITY AND NOT AN EMPLOYEE OR HIRED PERSON IN THE USUAL SENSE.

To Misconceive the Basic Nature and Role of the College or University Faculty Member Threatens the Whole Concept and Function of the Higher Learning.

In the long developmental history of the higher learning, the employer-employee relationship has been considered inappropriate for an academic community. A college or a university is fundamentally different from the business, military, or governmental organizations that so influence, indeed almost dominate, modern thought. The teacher-scholar (the faculty member) in an institution of higher learning is an "officer" of the corporation and in no meaningful sense is an employee (i.e., a man or woman hired to do a job as the employer wants it done).

In a college or university, the faculty members are responsible members of a self-governing community whose relative autonomy is crucial to the nature and process of the higher learning. This point is extremely complex and very difficult to make clear, yet on its acceptance may hang the welfare and perhaps even the survival of institutions of higher learning. The nature of the community of scholars has been developing for at least 800 years in the Western world and, in a sense, for the more than 2,000 years since Plato established his Academy. That nature involves the internal and external relationships that are fundamental to the purposes and processes of higher learning.

The crucial aspect of that relationship is that the individual faculty member is a self-respecting officer of the organization who, after proper evaluation by senior members of the community, becomes a permanent part of the organization, subject only to that community's requirement for excellence and integrity, such standards being administered by the community itself, including, of course, the lay board.

The complex concepts of academic freedom and tenure are related intricately to this principle. The status of the faculty member when this relation prevails is the very opposite of the hired man fighting for his rights. The effective administrator understands this principle, behaves in terms of it, and works diligently to help every member of the academic community to understand it.

To make this basic point about the role of the faculty member is not to ignore the apparently strong movement toward collective bargaining in higher education. Such bargaining for faculty contracts has up to now been confined largely to the community colleges, although some other institutions have elected organizations to represent them collectively. The issues involved in this process are extremely complex, and if Principle 14 is sound, of fundamental importance to the welfare and future of the higher learning.

Principle 15 Freedom

THE ADMINISTRATOR SHOULD PROTECT, ENCOURAGE, AND NOURISH FREEDOM WHENEVER POSSIBLE AS A QUALITY BASIC TO THE HIGHER LEARNING.

Freedom Is the Essence of the Higher Learning: To Achieve Genuine Individual and Group Freedom and To Learn the Wise Use of Freedom Are Important Purposes of the Higher Learning and the Essence of Its Process.

All possible freedom should be allowed for those working within the community of scholars, but the administrator should accept the responsibility for helping the community to set mutually agreed-upon limits. Freedom is the very lifeblood of the community of scholars. This freedom, so vital to the essence of higher learning, is perhaps more apparently important for the advanced work of the research university, where research and theoretical discussion on the very edge of knowledge are taking place, but, in reality, freedom is equally important for undergraduate learning and teaching. At best, the freedom should be in the nature of a spirit or an atmosphere that pervades the whole institution. The good administrator is constantly on guard to nourish and protect that freedom. He or she is sensitively alert to any beginning threats, from any source whatever, that may erode or dilute freedom. Immediately, a multitude of questions and problems arise to the thoughtful student of higher learning.

Freedom is never absolute. Every act performed by an individual affects others and, hence, involves their freedom. Even more important, freedom unrestrained rapidly goes to excess and not only harms others but destroys itself. The most desirable restraint, whether for the individual or a group, is self-restraint; but the self-restraint absolutely necessary to freedom requires a level of maturity that makes that kind of restraint possible. It follows, then, that the freedom necessary to the proper functioning of a community of scholars—an institution of higher learning—is possible only when the individuals, especially the faculty, but also the student body and the community as an organization, have the maturity requisite for such advanced freedom.

Here is probably the heart of the crisis of higher education in modern times—often, neither the faculty nor the student body has the maturity and the accompanying measure of self-restraint necessary to the freedom which is crucial to higher learning. The administrator understands this principle and, while nourishing and protecting freedom, leads the institution toward the understanding and the behavior that make freedom possible. In the meantime, he or she is greatly concerned that those who achieve tenure and become permanent members of the community have, or are achieving, a reasonable degree of maturity.

The administrator has a responsibility to preserve academic freedom from internal attacks. Threats to academic freedom were seen chiefly as external or administrative in origin until the late sixties. However, in more recent years the American Association of Universities has asserted that students and faculty members have also been responsible for violations of academic freedom.

Thus the administrator has a special responsibility to protect faculty members and students from intimidation as well as physical interference with their basic rights to conduct and attend classes in accord with institutional policies. Students also must be protected from coercion by faculty members by such means as prejudicial evaluation or exclusion from class because of philosophical differences with the faculty member.

The right to teach and the right to learn are firmly embedded in the tenets of academic freedom. The administrator has a responsibility to be watchful for both external and internal threats or attacks on the freedom necessary to the process of the higher learning.

Principle 16   Change and Stability

CHANGE, RENEWAL, AND CONSTANT READJUSTMENT ARE IMPORTANT ASPECTS OF THE VERY NATURE OF THE HIGHER LEARNING.

In a College or University, Constant Renewal and Growth within a Framework of Stability and Order Based upon the Nature and Purposes of the Higher Learning Become a Way of Life: a Continuous Process.

A balance between change and stability, between innovation and tradition, should be sought constantly. Man's attitude toward change and stability swings in wide arcs of time. At one time, the major emphasis will be upon change until the desire for innovation becomes almost compulsive; then, often without apparent reason, the chief concern is for stability.

Following World War II, a mood of change began building up, particularly in education, coming to a climax in the 1960s. The demand for innovation, of almost any kind and at any price, was urgent and persistent. The evidence seems to indicate that in the 1970s the emphasis moved back toward tradition or stability as educators searched for a desirable balance.

No one can completely escape the swings of fashion, whether in clothes or ideas, but the wise educational leader strives to avoid both extremes. He or she knows that change, a characteristic of growth, is the very nature of life. However, as a student of mankind and of history, he or she does not expect or wish sudden leaps of progress. One remembers that all, or nearly all, significant and good change is the result of growth that, as a rule, cannot be rushed or forced.

At the same time, the administrator should be sensitive to the wide range of faculty responses to the prospect of change, especially when it is sudden, unexpected, or is or seems to be external in origin. The method of the introduction of change, as well as the timing of the announcement, can affect profoundly the potential acceptance of the innovation.

The administrator, rather than making a fetish of immediate innovation or of tradition, aims to create a climate of renewal or innovation which will help the college or university to stimulate and to deal with change in such a way as to profit from the best that has been learned in the past without being enslaved by that past.

The goal is to make the college or university a place of continuous, healthy, but not cancerous or artificial growth—a place where renewal is a way of life.

Principle 17   Attitudes toward Youth

RESPECT AND LISTEN TO YOUTH, BUT DO NOT SURRENDER TO THEM OR BE AFRAID OF THEM.

Administrators Tend To Go To Extremes in Their Attitudes Toward Youth: from Antagonism and Suspicion to Unrealistic Confidence and Expectation. Youth Should Be Respected for Freshness and Spontaneity, and Restrained and Guided because of Inexperience: Balance Is the Key.

The youth of college and university age are to be respected, but not feared; and their originality or significance neither should be over-valued nor undervalued. The administrator is in danger of going to one of two extremes, either of which would hamper his effectiveness. On the one hand, he or she may be awed and cowed by the freshness and appealing audacity of youth. The result of this attitude is an inability to stand up to the pristine naiveté of those whose ideas never have faced the test of reality. The other extreme is to discount or resist out-of-hand the ideas and ideals of youth, saying in effect that there is nothing new here—"We tried that ten years ago and it didn't work"— and thus refuse to listen to voices that have not been muted or distorted yet by the failures or hardships common to life. Both of these extremes can be avoided.

The wise administrator learns to listen sincerely, without allowing his or her own perception and judgment to be warped. It seems that, in recent times, the greater danger is that the administrator will be overinfluenced or even afraid of the strong-minded and articulate young. Many adults, particularly modern parents, appear to be incapable of standing up to young people in the way that is probably best for their learning and development.

Often, an otherwise mature administrator takes an indefensible position because his or her son or daughter has had trouble in the area involved. Such behavior may be human, but it is a great threat to an administrator's effectiveness and to the institution. The application of this principle requires close, continuous, and respectful relations with the students of the academic community—balance in that relationship is the key.

A faithful recognition of student diversity is crucial to the wise application of this principle. Administrators—and faculty members—must be sensitive to change in student characteristics. The majority of institutions are experiencing significant changes in the characteristics of students; many of the common assumptions related to the "average" students are being subjected to serious scrutiny. For example, proportionately more women are entering college; more students are employed part-time or full time; the average age of students is rising. Adequate knowledge and understanding of the meaning of these changes are important for the administrator and the faculty.

Principle 18   Students and Academic Governance

STUDENTS ARE A CRUCIAL PART OF THE ACADEMIC COMMUNITY: THEY CAN BE AN IMPORTANT PART OF THE GOVERNING PROCESS OF THE COLLEGE OR UNIVERSITY.

Students Can Make a Significant Contribution to Effective Governance of Colleges and Universities. Since No Generally Accepted Model Has Been Worked Out for the Optimum Place of Students in Governance, Administration Will Be Breaking New Ground in This Area. Student Participation Can Be a Vital Part of the Educative Process.

Perhaps one of the least productive and creative aspects of the academic community is what is commonly called student government. Here is a problem still largely unsolved. There has been much change since the old authoritarian times of the colonial college, which remained as a basic model through most of the 19th century, but evidently a good solution for the creative use of students in governing and carrying on the work of the community of scholars has not been found. There are institutional exceptions, but in the main, the role of students leaves them isolated, not fully used, often resentful and bitter. This problem will challenge the ingenuity and skill of the very best administrator.

The reasons for the extreme difficulty of the problem are fairly clear. Whitehead summarizes the deep issues well in this statement:

> The tragedy of the world is that those who are imaginative have but slight experience, and those who are experienced have feeble imaginations. Fools act on imagination without knowledge; pedants act on knowledge without imagination. The task of a university is to weld together imagination and experience.
>
> The initial discipline of imagination in its period of youthful vigor requires that there be no responsibility for immediate action.

It is natural, one supposes, that adults carrying heavy responsibility for which they must take the consequences resent the rash, sometimes arrogant, ways of youth unsobered by experience. But youth is equally impatient with the often deadening effect of experience where imagination and spontaneity have lost their place and power. Here is the essence of the generation gap which is present seemingly in the very nature of life, and thus is best faced squarely. Surely a way can be found to combine the two planes of life as Whitehead suggests. No person who has tried to rear a family or to operate a school at any level, particularly a college or university, will be naive enough to expect an early solution.

Even so, we venture a few suggestions. The first is that administrators consciously strive to overcome natural adult prejudices and fears, and learn to respect the special strengths and abilities of youth. In achieving this respect one must avoid two extremes: the old view that basically youth is inevitably irresponsible and bent upon no good; the equally foolish notion that youth is the repository of a pristine, unspoiled wisdom not to be thwarted. The truth lies somewhere between these extremes; its perception and use depend much upon mutual respect.

The administrator should find a dependable means of having close and continuous contact with genuine representatives of the student body. Because we have yet to find a generally acceptable model for academic governments, official representatives are a special type of person often representing a narrow segment of the student body. But even so, regular contact with them is highly valuable.

There is strong argument that a direct meeting with representative students in larger groups with the president or dean or department chairman on a regularly scheduled basis is much more productive than having student representatives in committees or councils, however democratic it may seem. In this case, both the students and the faculty tend to become defensive and the best interchange is often lost. Both methods doubtless may be useful.

Space permits only one other point on an issue that deserves a volume. Since we have no ideal model for academic governance, it is no marvel that we have not been able to bring the students effectively into the governance. There have been many successes by individual presidents and deans built largely upon the individual style of the administrators, and, frankly, the evidence indicates, to some at least, that the wise, enlightened use of the family model has been more successful in fully using the abilities and talents of the students; for example, Wheeler at his best at Berkeley. *University Authority and the Student: The Berkeley Experience*, Otten's excellent study, is highly recommended.

A final general word may be useful: The administrator should remember that the institution operates primarily for the education of the students. Even in the case of advanced professional or research functions, the learning and modeling of the student is of crucial importance. Thus a conscious and studied attempt should be made to involve students in the process of the institution, not only or even perhaps primarily because they can be very useful, but even more because their mere participation can be a crucial part of the education process at all levels of the higher learning. It might be said that any task a student can do reasonably well without too much risk to the welfare of the institution, should be done by the student.

Principle 19   Diversity and Variety in Thought and Behavior

DIVERSITY AND VARIATION IN THOUGHT AND EVEN IN BEHAVIOR ARE TO BE RESPECTED AND ENCOURAGED WITHIN THE MUTUALLY ACCEPTED STANDARDS OF THE ACADEMIC COMMUNITY.

Independence of Mind Often Expressed in Diversity Is the Life Blood of the Process of the Higher Learning: The Common Tendency of Organizations To Demand Conformity Must Be Resisted and Guarded Against: The Good Administrator Accepts, Respects, and Even Encourages Variety.

Diversity and variety among staff, faculty, board, and students should be accepted and respected. A chief characteristic of the members of a community of scholars is independence of mind. Variety of opinion not only is tolerated but is encouraged.

The academic community has its self-established standards of behavior and human relations, but these are conceived broadly so as to permit varied approaches to problems. This variety is often an annoyance to the administrator who, by nature, feels better when people behave as he or she does. Here we are in the realm of style, which probably is rooted in temperament. Individuals develop personal styles from early youth and, by the time they become a part of an academic community, particularly as a faculty or board member, their manner of behavior is relatively fixed.

Attitudes in faculty meetings, in classroom or laboratory, in personal or group conference, even on social occasions, reflect this deeply fixed style of life. Often the behavior may be, or may seem to be, relatively irrational, eccentric, even bizarre. Of course, behavior, dress, or language may become so different or unusual that the faculty member's usefulness as a scholar-teacher is damaged or, in extreme cases, may be such as to disqualify the person for membership in the community. More often, the variation is simply unpleasant or embarrassing.

The wise administrator learns to expect this wide variety of personality and behavior in a community that takes pride in independence of thought and does not become unduly disturbed, but seeks to understand and work constructively with the individual, disregarding as much as possible the latter's annoying surface eccentricities.

Principle 20   Economy

THERE IS NEVER ENOUGH MONEY.

Since Resources Are Always Finite or Limited, a Prime Problem of Any Organization is To Establish and Administer Priorities That Reflect the Longtime Welfare of the Whole: The Administrator Must Constantly State and Interpret the Basic Principle of Economy.

Special effort should be made to help every person who is a part of the institution to be sensitively aware of the crucial importance of money, since nothing is more certain to destroy a college or university than inefficient or careless financial management. There is a tendency for faculty, staff, and students to feel that institutional finance is not their problem, that the financial well-being of the institution is the problem of the administration and the board.

Faculty, staff, and students often say as much. This attitude arises, at least in part, from a neglect to inform them and to help them to understand and be keenly concerned about the financial health of the institution.

Prolonged indifference or scorn toward financial problems results in a division of the academic community into two more or less contending groups. Members of one group strive to get all of the available resources possible for themselves personally or, at least, for their programs; the others take the stance that it is their chief responsibility to protect the resources from grasping and largely irresponsible persons. In such an unhealthy climate the quality and general welfare of the whole institution suffer.

The task of the administrator is to help all to see and to believe that the financial stability of the college or university is of utmost importance to all who are a part of it; that resources always are limited and, hence, priorities must be established for their use; and that money improperly used or wasted deprives some part of the institution.

Not all members of the academic community will have the wisdom to accept this principle and to live by it, but we often underestimate people's ability to believe in an institution, to work diligently for it, and even to sacrifice for its genuine welfare. There is much untapped loyalty in faculties and student bodies.

Principle 21   Financial Accountability

EVERY PROGRAM IN THE INSTITUTION SHOULD BE REQUIRED CONTINUOUSLY TO JUSTIFY ITS USE OF THE INSTITUTION'S RESOURCES.

Perhaps Not Every Program Can or Should Bear Its Own Weight Financially, but Its Cost Should Clearly Be Known and the Justification of That Cost in Terms of the Institution's Purposes Should Be Convincing and Clear and Re-examined at Regular Intervals.

Every aspect of the institution, as much as possible, should bear its own weight, financially and psychologically. It was very interesting and instructive to see this point emphasized in a recent report by the president of Harvard University. This first, and now wealthiest, of our colleges and universities has the greatest financial and psychological resources of any of our institutions of higher learning. Yet, apparently, Harvard long has operated on the principle that each program and organizational unit of the institution should be financially responsible and, as near as possible, self-supporting. Evidently, some programs attract less financial support than others, and some are proportionally much more expensive. Also, a beginning program which eventually may be financially sound may require subsidy in the early stages. It is easy for these facts to become excuses for asking the rest of the institution to carry dead or dying programs, or to subsidize the lack of initiative and energy of those responsible for a particular program.

The economic viability of a program should not be the crucial deciding factor, but this should be carefully considered and, if a program does not attract adequate support and resources over a period of time, the matter should be studied with great care. Few things are more destructive of morale than that one part of an institution is, or is thought to be, carrying the weight of another part.

Closely related is the need to justify clearly and regularly the phases of the institution that often are called overhead—administration, student services, and the like. There is a tendency for administrative organization to proliferate. The question must be asked constantly: Are these offices bearing their own weight in the organization? If so, how are they related to the major purposes of the institution? This problem requires the availability of adequate facts and the constant interpretation of them to the whole institution.

Principle 22   Responsible Speech and Writing

THE ADMINISTRATOR BOTH IN PUBLIC AND PRIVATE MUST SPEAK AND WRITE WITH CARE AND RESTRAINT: THE OFFICER'S WORDS INEVITABLY REPRESENT THE OFFICE.

The Administrator Longs To Be Free, but Reasonable Restraint and Care Are a Part of His or Her Responsibility. Words Written or Spoken in Private, in Confidence, or Even in Jest Have a Way of Appearing in Public Out of Context and Often Distorted: The Need To Say the Smart Thing That May Seem Especially Apt About a

Person or a Problem Is Very Great for the Administrator: Reliable Confidants Are Very Rare.

The spirit and practice of freedom are the essence of the higher learning. Every member of the academic community, the college or university, wishes to be free. But the relatively mature person learns to face the fact that there is no absolute freedom in life. Certain positions or offices inevitably carry with them special restraints. The physician does not, and one judges does not wish to, speak freely or publicly about a patient. And so with many professional men and women: lawyers, ministers, accountants, etc. College or university administrators are no exception. When they assume an administrative responsibility, a corresponding responsibility for restraint in expression is assumed.

Some administrators resent and resist any restraint on their personal freedom. This attitude is understandable but may lead to trouble. It is inevitable that there is a tendency to confuse the office a person holds with the person. What an administrator says or writes will always represent the office to some degree, however carefully the person may emphasize that he or she is speaking as an individual. When the administrator's words are quoted or repeated they will be interpreted as being from the department chairman, or the dean, or the president. This point is not intended to put a damper on frankness or forthrightness: It is simply a counsel to be aware of reality and to be prepared for its consequences.

There is a more subtle issue, but it must be sensed almost intuitively and hence cannot easily be made clear on the formal intellectual level. The administrator needs to be free, at ease, reasonably unrestrained. There will be an inclination to seek that ease among a few confidants, in some social situation, and especially among the family. But words spoken in the most private and confidential relations have a way of being noised abroad, and if they are about persons, or even sensitive issues, they appear in public distorted. The administrator is likely to have keen perceptions which can be expressed easily, and the need to express them is sometimes almost uncontrollable. If strong, this trait can disqualify an administrator. A single, witty characterization of an influential, sensitive person may cost dearly in later relations. It has been suggested that a private characterization of Senator Lodge by

President Wilson may have adversely affected the fate of the League of Nations.

We hesitate to write of this principle because it is so likely to be misunderstood. The last thing we would argue for is a timid, over-restrained administrator full of fear and hesitancy. Caution and careful common sense in speech and writing, remembering that what one says will be considered an expression of the office held, do not seem to be seriously inhibiting principles. Nor should one who wants to hold responsibility refuse to face the fact that there are very few instances where there is genuine confidentiality: What an administrator says is likely to be repeated. These are characteristic aspects of holding special positions. Some people will argue that one should say or write nothing that he or she would not be glad to have repeated or even printed. That is a high, perhaps unreasonable, standard to set for most mortals.

The effective administrator searches for and eventually finds a suitable and satisfying style and practice in this area. It is very helpful if the administrator can have a few confidants with whom there can be total freedom: Such relations will be rare. For some temperaments, reasonable and wise restraint is easy; for others, restraint is a constant battle. Perhaps the latter should consider retiring to the remarkable freedom of the faculty member, although even there speech and writing cannot be wholly free. Faculty members' irresponsible comments about students, colleagues, or administrators have the potential to injure and embarrass both parties to the comments.

Principle 23   Mistakes

FACE MISTAKES SQUARELY BUT DO NOT MAKE TOO MANY: TO ERR IS HUMAN, BUT TO ERR WHEN A LITTLE FORETHOUGHT OR CARE WOULD HAVE AVOIDED THE MISTAKE RAPIDLY UNDERMINES CONFIDENCE.

Few Things Affect Administrators More Than Their Method or Style in Dealing With Mistakes Which Are an Inevitable Part of Any Organization: To Be Defensive and Play the Omnipotent Role Is Abrasive and May Be Fatal; To Hide behind the Human Tendency for Error Is Equally Destructive: A Balanced Way Is Hard To Follow but Surely Not Impossible.

College administrators should not be afraid to acknowledge and correct mistakes. They may go to either of two extremes with respect to this principle. Probably they are more likely, because of the nature of the office, to assume, consciously or unconsciously, the attitude of omnipotence and resist strenuously all indications that they might have made a mistake. This defensiveness may manifest itself in flatly denying that an error has been made or in attempting to place the blame on someone else. The strong need in such cases is to appear to be perfect, or nearly so.

The other extreme is equally damaging to administrators and the institutions where they carry responsibility. In this case, the administrator makes a "technique" of acknowledging and taking responsibility for mistakes. The attitude is that no one is perfect and so it is good to face one's mistakes, for then people will tend to overlook them and, in a sense, the errors become a strength.

The wise way lies somewhere between these two extremes. Administrators cannot blandly accept blame for all errors, or all that any critic may consider as an error. Then they will soon be discredited. Perhaps administrators should frankly accept and face clearcut mistakes, but the crucial point is that they must not make very many serious errors, for then no amount of acceptance of the blame will save them. A recent historical incident, much publicized, will illustrate this point: The Bay of Pigs incident was serious; President John Kennedy's honesty and courage in facing the mistake and accepting responsibility for it strengthened him with the American public; the necessity of facing very many such mistakes would have rapidly undermined confidence in his skill and judgment. The administrator should have the courage to acknowledge and correct mistakes, but too many such mistakes must not be made.

Principle 24   Institutional Tradition and Practice

LEARN, RESPECT, AND WORK WITHIN THE TRADITIONS AND ESTABLISHED PRACTICES OF THE INSTITUTION.

In a Sense, Colleges and Universities Are Very Conservative Insti-

tutions. Though Theoretically Open to New Ideas and Drastic Changes, These Institutions Embody and Work in Terms of Very Old Tradition and Long-Established Practice. Every Separate Institution Has a Special Character or Personality Which Must Be Respected and Changed with Care and Wisdom.

When an administrator assumes a new position, he or she would be wise to take ample time to study the situation carefully before undertaking major changes. This principle may be applied somewhat differently if the person assuming the new responsibility is from within the organization, has had long experience with the problems of the institution, and has won the respect of colleagues upon whose cooperation the success of the endeavor will depend. To undertake broad and deep changes without adequate knowledge of the local circumstances and without the respect of one's peers is to court disaster.

It might be argued that the newly appointed administrator should take advantage of the newness and the relative goodwill and cooperativeness that usually accompany a new administrator, a time when mistakes are overlooked and opposition is reduced by an aura of good feeling. There may be special occasions or circumstances when it is wise to drive hard toward specific goals of reorganization or achievement during these early months, but the evidence seems to suggest that such situations are the exception. The rule is to take time to get the facts and win confidence.

An institution of higher learning, even a relatively new one—the same is true of a department or a school or college—operates in terms of many counterbalancing forces, including the very strong power of tradition and long-prevailing practice. Beyond the relatively specific and observable factors, a college or university has what best can be characterized as a personality or character or way of doing things.

Effectively carrying on the operation—not to speak of deep, far-reaching change such as Eliot effected at Harvard—must take into account and use the basic spirit of the institution. An administrator attempting to move rapidly in terms of his or her preconception and ambition—even though, in themselves, they may be good—is likely to encounter increasing trouble, and often may be sincerely baffled by the forces that persistently hinder and destroy the effort.

Principle 25   Campus Guests
THE TREATMENT OF GUESTS ON CAMPUS REFLECTS
THE SPIRIT OF THE INSTITUTION AS A WHOLE.

*The Care of Official and Even Unofficial Guests on Campus
Should Express Both the Spirit and Efficiency of the Institution: The
Administrator Will Need To Delegate Much of the Detailed Plan-
ning and Work, but Effectiveness and Courtesy in Carrying Out the
Plan Will Finally Be the Responsibility of the Administrator.*

Careful, detailed plans should be made for the comfort and con-
venience of people who are invited to the campus for special occasions or services. The administrator may wish to delegate this responsibility, depending upon the nature of the occasion and the identity of
the visitor, but often, particularly in smaller institutions, he or she
may wish to have a personal part in the plans and their execution.

Be that as it may, the point is that careful plans should be made for
all official visitors. These persons may range from an incidental
lecturer for a special event to the speaker for a graduation program or
other all-school occasion. The significance of the principle lies in the
fact that the way a guest is planned for and dealt with tends to show
how the whole institution operates: whether things go smoothly or
are confused or drag. Those who have visited a variety of institutions
as speakers or on accreditation teams, etc. will have observed how
widely colleges and universities vary in their treatment of visitors.

The most effective institutions plan with care every aspect of the
visitor's stay, including travel arrangements, escorts about the campus, guidance to the specific program, and living accommodations,
taking care not to over-schedule for social or other events. These
institutions seem to sense what arrangements will lift from the visitor
the anxieties and irritants arising from making the decisions asso-
ciated with being in a strange place. Thus, the guest is free to be his or
her best self and the institution manifests a quality of hospitality and
relaxed planning that reveals its deeper nature and helps it to grow
toward what it wishes to be.

The other extreme is the institution that allows official guests to
fend for themselves even to the point of finding parking and wander-

ing more or less lost about the campus until time for the program to begin.

In many cases students and younger faculty members can be effectively used as hosts and hostesses. An institution has a personality: Few things reveal the nature of personality more deeply than how one deals with guests.

Principle 26 Gossip and Pressure

LISTEN AND LEARN, BUT MAKE UP YOUR OWN MIND.

A College or University, in Spite of Its High Purposes and Long Tradition, Is a Very Human Community Subject Almost as Much as Any Group to Gossip, Rumor, and Pressure: The Good Administrator Guards against and Carefully Makes Allowances for This Influence in Making Decisions.

The administrator should not be influenced unduly by campus gossip and propaganda. Most of what is passed around in the category of "Did you know?..." is not true or is a distorted report of a partial truth. A college or university community seems to be especially subject to the creation and dissemination of rumor, a strange fact in view of the training and high calling of the community of scholars.

The dean of instruction or of faculty—often now designated vice-president of academic affairs—perhaps needs to be more alert to this principle than does the president. There will be waves of gossip-generated sentiment for or against a faculty member which may distort the facts badly and, in turn, confuse an important decision. Criticism may begin running against a faculty member and students and many faculty colleagues may get on the bandwagon. Due to the strange power of words, almost without regard to their source, a seriously negative report listened to or read tends to lodge in the mind and to influence his or her attitude. "Did you know that Professor Jones is a little dictator in his classes?" One knows that it is not true, yet when Professor Jones is met on campus, there is a slightly different feeling about him.

The administrator needs a steady head not to be over-influenced by rumor, especially if it is, or seems to be, widespread. A very small group—ten or twenty on a campus of several thousand—which is persistent can give the impression of representing a broadly based feeling. Such gossip may be either positive (to support a prize or a tenure appointment) or it may be negative (to destroy a person, a program, or even a school). At the same time, the administrator must not be stubbornly blind to gossip or rumor, for it may point to something important that should be known.

Principle 27 The Danger of Crowd Psychology

AVOID MOB SITUATIONS OR THOSE THAT LEND THEM-SELVES TO THE PSYCHOLOGY OF THE CROWD AS MUCH AS POSSIBLE.

The Effectiveness of the Rational Process Seems To Be Inversely Related to the Size of the Group Involved: The Larger the Group the More Likely Emotion and Crowd Spirit Will Prevail. The Good Administrator Strives To See That Important Academic Business Is Done in Relatively Small Properly Constituted Groups.

The business of an institution can be carried on most effectively in small groups, as a rule. Perhaps Emerson overstated the principle somewhat, but he was not far from the mark when he said that two people are nearly always sincere, but, upon the entrance of a third, they all three become hypocrites.

The degree to which reason and openness to evidence can prevail seems to be related to the size of the group—the larger the group, the more the individuals succumb to the mob spirit of psychology, which is both treacherous and dangerous. Demagogues seem to perceive and use this principle almost instinctively. The most bizarre example within the memory of many now living is that of Hitler speaking to a huge audience of reasonably intelligent German people, leading them to thought and action which, as individuals or families, they hardly would have considered.

An example from the institution the writers serve may help to make the point clearer. Throughout the turbulent and often irrational 1960s, the University of Southern California had held its balance remarkably well. There were tensions, of course, for the feverish emotion was pervasive, but nothing significant enough to threaten the university's normal and legitimate processes. Then came the incident at Kent State University and related events. A few ardent and highly emotional people called for a general assembly of faculty, students, and administration, and such a meeting was called. The meeting was in no sense legal or official. In spite of a sincere and skillful chairman, the assembly was a mob. Rational thought was scarce and, when it appeared, largely disdained.

These examples may be extreme, but the principle is basic—the administrator as much as he or she can, should avoid trying to carry on the business of the institution in large groups. If the wish is to inspire or to inform, large groups may be useful, but for thought or decision based on evidence, they are useless or, in some cases, even dangerous.

Principle 28   Foresight or Prometheus

TO SEE AND PLAN AHEAD IS THE ESSENCE OF WISDOM.

Many Problems Can Be Easily Solved in Their Early Manifestations, but if Allowed To Build Up and Fester Become Seriously Disruptive: The Wise Administrator Strives to See Ahead and if Possible Nip the Problem in the Bud.

The administrator should strive to anticipate, as much as possible, the need for change and development. Wisdom often lies in foresight. It is remarkably better to see what should be done and to begin doing it before pressure develops to force the action.

Thomas Mann, the great German novelist, in his insightful series of novels about Joseph, illustrates again and again that the essence of wisdom lies in "seeing before" and in acting in terms of that foresight. The point is made most powerfully in his *Joseph The Provider*. Here, the farseeing alien prime minister saves his adopted country by seeing ahead what should be done and doing it with skill.

Perhaps not many administrators can hope to have the divine guidance or perceptive genius of Joseph. The administrator does not need these special abilities in great measure in order to apply this principle. As a rule, there are evident things that need to be done in an institution of higher learning. For various reasons, not the least of which is the tendency to do only that which one is pushed to do, these needs remain unmet, build up in intensity, and eventually present serious problems.

One only has to walk over the typical campus to see many physical conditions that need attention. Those involving human relations, academic procedures, and communications failures are doubtless more difficult to perceive, although they are, of course, more serious for the welfare of the institution. These errors and neglects are usually the result of a failure to see what is taking place and what the consequences are likely to be—the result of a policy of drift.

One sees the violation of this principle most clearly in the general society. Willa Cather vividly describes the basic evil in our prison system in *O, Pioneers!* (1913). The situation drifted to the demoralizing riots of 1971, and to the present. The neglect of prison conditions, the ill-treatment of minorities and women, tax inequities, and environmental pollution are examples of failure to see relatively evident problems. The good administrator, with the assistance of all in the community of scholars, learns to see conditions that need attention in their early stages and works to remedy them.

Principle 29   Power of the Administrative Office

THE OFFICE HAS GREAT POWER AND PRESTIGE: THE PRESENT OCCUPANT HAS ONLY LIMITED POWER.

The Academic Community Is Very Sensitive to Process and Is Basically Democratic in Spirit: The Wise Administrator Uses the Power of the Office With Careful Restraint: Victories Ruthlessly Achieved Often Prove Pyrrhic.

The power of the administrator's office should be used with care. There is great temptation to use that power to push an action through a board, a faculty, or even a committee. An action passed over the strong opposition of sincere and deeply interested persons is often an expensive victory.

The administrator may have committed himself or herself prematurely to a particular action, and may feel that, if it is not followed through as planned, face will be lost; the administrator may have thought about and studied the issue over a long period of time, and may judge the readiness of others to act in terms of that feeling. Whatever the cause of the feeling of urgency, it is usually unwise to push through a decision over sincere and informed opposition. If one knows that he or she has the votes to pass a measure, the temptation is great to try to save time or to get the matter settled. Usually, a little more time for thought and discussion will win over the more thoughtful opposition.

This principle does not suggest that a consensus can or always should be achieved, but it does suggest that relatively evenly split votes on important issues are a signal that trouble is ahead. The effective administrator senses this danger and works patiently and diligently to avoid bitter division, especially if there is a good chance that time and further evidence will avoid it.

There are exceptions, of course, to this approach. There are times when an issue needs to be settled, when a measure needs to be adopted, even by a thin margin. Then, the administrator may do all that he or she considers fair and wise to get the votes. The point is that these occasions should be rare. If the opposition is large and the issue is vital, the narrow victory may cost dearly in later relations.

Principle 30 Pacing Activity

THE PACE AND RHYTHM OF THE ADMINISTRATOR'S ACTIVITY SHOULD BE ADJUSTED TO PERSONAL TEMPERAMENT AS WELL AS TO THE DEMANDS OF THE JOB.

The Light, Relaxed Touch is Very Important to Effective Administration: The Over-Busy, Harassed Administrator Endangers His or Her Own Effectiveness and Health and Creates an Atmosphere of Tension and Distrust.

The administrator's work is a cross-country run, not a 100-yard dash. The administrator must develop a style of administration that fits his or her temperament, a pace and rhythm of work that allow the maximum achievement with a minimum of wasted energy. The typical training for administration seems to help very little in this area. The chief reason may lie in the fact that self-understanding is extremely hard to achieve.

Many of the administrators whom we have known personally seem essentially slaves to their jobs. Their typical response to an inquiry about how they are getting along is: "Terribly busy and pressed." The impression is that the position is working them, instead of the reverse. Many seem to be running as fast as they can, sometimes in the wrong direction. The conviction appears to be that, if they could just increase their speed, all would be well.

This 100-yard dash attitude manifests itself in many ways, but three common ones will suffice for illustration—the neglect of broad reading, failure to take proper recreation, and the tendency to isolate oneself from many of the responsibilities of the job. Modern administrators often claim that they lack time to read and, particularly, time to write. If time were made for regular reading, and even for reading in depth in the area of chief interest, administrators might find their perspective greatly increased.

Proper recreation often is seriously neglected, resulting in staleness and increased irritability. Regular recreation appropriate to individual temperament would contribute much to the continuous renewal so necessary for health and effectiveness on the job. The tendency for an administrator to be isolated in a shell of "busy-ness" is usually a culmination of the prolonged use of a style of work which is tension-producing. An appropriate style enables the administrator to bring the light touch to all effort, so the more that is accomplished, the less busy the person seems to be. The job, then, even though very demanding, may become a creative fulfillment.

Principle 31   Decisiveness

EVEN A BAD DECISION MAY BE BETTER THAN VACIL-LATION: RISK IS A PART OF GOOD ADMINISTRATION.

The Good Administrator Must Be Decisive without Being Rash and Precipitant: There Comes a Time When Indecision Destroys Confidence and Fosters Division: To Recognize That Moment and To Act Decisively Is a Trait of the Effective Administrator.

The administrator should avoid both the appearance and the reality of being indecisive. We emphasize here one aspect of decision-making, i.e., the individual administrator's skill in being, and appearing to be, able to make up his or her mind without violating, or seeming to violate, the academic community's very sensitive feelings of due process.

In this area, the administrator is between two powerful forces, and constantly is in danger of being crushed by them. There is the steady pressure or decision: "What is holding things up? That proposal has been on the president's desk for weeks. Can't the man make a decision?" On the other side comes an equal pressure. The president or other administrator makes up his or her mind quickly and acts on the decision. Thus, the needed action is kept going, but often there is a cry against this kind of administrator—that he or she is dictatorial, authoritarian, arbitrary, even ruthless.

There must be a way out of this vexing dilemma. The way, if there is one, involves so much subtle common sense and personal style, rooted in temperament, that worthwhile practical suggestions are very difficult to give. One basic principle may be helpful—as a rule, although there are exceptions, the specific choice in a given decision is not nearly as important as making the decision and then following through promptly and wisely.

Indecisiveness multiplies problems; precipitous unilateral decisions offend the academic community. The administrator must make decisions; he or she must follow due process with care; and must find a certain joy or zest in walking this knife's edge.

Principle 32 Successful Striving and Morale

PERCEIVABLE PROGRESS TOWARD AGREED-UPON GOALS IS CRUCIAL TO GOOD MORALE IN A COLLEGE OR UNIVERSITY.

Immediate and Long-time Goals Accepted and Understood by the Individuals Who Make Up the Community of Scholars Give Purpose, Direction, and Zest to Both Individuals and the Group: The Good Administrator Sees That There Is Progress toward These Goals, and That the Progress Is Known—That Striving Is Successful.

The institution should have clear and achievable goals toward which it is moving perceptibly. Few things strengthen an institution, or a person, like successful striving. Because of the special emphasis upon financial stress in recent years, attention has been placed largely upon forward movement in the financial area. The administrators who have been able to keep a building program going and, particularly, to keep faculty salaries on the rise, almost even with inflation, have been able to survive.

There was the impression of real forward movement even if, in the long run, the reality was more like running very hard to keep up. Often, more buildings, increased faculty salaries, and rapidly expanded enrollments increased costs, and eventually brought the institution or the system to a financial crisis. The point is that any kind of forward movement unifies and strengthens for a time, but if it is basically apparent rather than real the reckoning day will come—as it will for an individual or a family living beyond its income—and the consequences may be severe. This danger should not deter the administrator from an attempt to lead physical and financial forward movement. Indeed, such movement, reasonably solidly based, is crucial.

At the same time, there should be a constant search for progress—positive goals—in the less physical areas, which often need not involve extra outlays of money. Rather, they involve imagination and persistent effort, which are frequently in shorter supply than money: meaningful goals and movement toward them in the curriculum, programs for the improvement of teaching and learning, governance so as to provide wider participation, better working and living conditions, more opportunity for discussion of issues, increased training of faculty, various kinds of community service—the list can be very long. Achievement in these areas gives a quality of life, growth, and forward movement to the institution. The administrator cannot, and should not, do these things alone or push too hard for them, but, as a rule, must be a key stimulator.

Principle 33 Faculty and Staff Discussion
THE ADMINISTRATOR SHOULD RESTRAIN THE NATURAL TENDENCY TO SPEAK TOO MUCH OR TO DOMINATE THE DISCUSSION PROCESS.

When Discussion Leading toward a Decision Is in Process It Is of Utmost Importance That the Exchange Be Open and Free: An Administrator Who Is a Part of the Discussion Group Is Often Tempted To Dominate the Discussion because of Habit or Temperament.

When a decision is in process, the administrator should take care not to dominate the discussion by talking too much. Perhaps too much talk on the part of anyone is harmful, but the administrator is subject to a special danger on this point.

Of course, there is a time to take a strong stand, and it may be important to make this position clear before general sentiment becomes crystallized or begins running in a direction that may be irreversible. Yet, when a problem is being debated in committee or by a larger group, it will be wise, as a rule, for the administrator to refrain from entering the discussion. As far as possible, while adhering to the principles of sincerity and integrity, he or she should remain above the immediate struggle.

Catherine Drinker Bowen's *Miracle at Philadelphia* gives a vivid picture of George Washington at the Constitutional Convention. He was clearly the most highly respected, and perhaps the most influential, man there. It is remarkable how little he spoke—how wisely and subtly he used silence—in the urgent and often heated debates of the Convention. Recent biographies reveal the same trait in Thomas Jefferson, who also was a skillful and wise administrator. He, too, had the ability to hold his words to a minimum when decisions were in process.

Evidently, there is a time to speak and there is a time to be silent. The effective administrator strives for a balanced wisdom, which always must reflect his or her genuine style. Holding one's tongue simply as a technique is artificial and, in the long run, will undermine confidence. To be effective, the remaining above the immediate struggle must be a true reflection of the nature of the person.

Administrative decisions take much of their shape and quality from the information available to the administrator. Faculty members are often more willing to express in speech rather than other forms of communication their concerns and perceptions. Consequently, thoughtful listening is a basic skill in acquiring and sorting information. There is, of course, a danger in passive listening. Silence on an issue may be interpreted as tacit approval of the speaker's views. Thus, the listener, especially the administrator, must be wary of having implied agreement by being silent, when such apparent agreement may introduce a secondary problem in the future.

Principle 34   Trusted Counselors of the Administrator

THE ADMINISTRATOR SHOULD HAVE AN INNER CIR-CLE OF TRUSTED COUNSELORS, BUT SHOULD SEEK AND LEARN TO LISTEN TO A VARIETY OF VIEWS.

The Administrator Needs a Trusted Inner Set of Counselors Where Discussion Is Open, Free, and Characterized by Mutual Respect: There Is Always Serious Danger That Such an Inner Circle Will Become Closed, Over-protective, and Resistant to Crucial Facts—a Sure Road to Trouble.

An inner corps of broadly representative but loyal advisers who, within council, are free and able to voice their sincere and confidential opinions is very valuable to an administrator. One of the greatest hazards to administrators is the strong tendency to become isolated, and thus to hear only what they want to hear or, equally harmful, that which those around them want them to hear.

Probably no important principle is easy to apply, but this one involves particularly subtle psychological issues. A person who carries heavy responsibility has a great, almost instinctive, need to be surrounded with people who have similar attitudes, which often means individuals with like backgrounds, values, and even methods of approaching problems. Such a group, especially as an inner circle, creates comfort and confidence. Any person in first authority needs a measure of such a supporting environment, but it may be bought at a disastrously high price. Baldly stated, that price is ignorance of important facts and points of view crucial to a clear picture of the problem at hand.

The administrator may be deprived of aspects of the truth—the nature of the situation—that a person who must make a decision needs desperately. History probably will reveal that the series of strange mistakes which a succession of U.S. Presidents made in Southeast Asia resulted from this kind of isolation from vital information and varied views.

At the same time, one must face the fact that a diversity in council may have a disconcerting and weakening effect. An ancient text warns that he who looks at the clouds never will sow—he who considers all contingencies will never act—but, in the absence of intuitive insight approaching genius, which is rare, not to look carefully is to risk serious mistakes.

Principle 35   The Administrative Office and the Person Who Temporarily Occupies the Office

THE ADMINISTRATIVE OFFICE HAS MUCH MEANING, POWER, AND OFTEN PRESTIGE, WHICH ARE NOT TO BE CONFUSED WITH THE PERSON WHO TEMPORARILY OCCUPIES THE OFFICE.

There Is a Strong, Natural Tendency for the Person Who Occupies an Administrative Office To Believe and Behave as if He or She Were the Office: a Mistake To Be Avoided Diligently.

The office of the administrator—president, dean, department chairman, etc.—should be valued, protected, and enriched without overemphasis on the person who occupies the office. Sophocles made this observation in *Antigone*:

> But hard it is to learn
> The mind of any mortal or the heart
> Till he be tried in chief authority.
> Power shows the man.

Every college administrator should read these lines now and then and ponder what his or her administrative office is revealing. Not only does power show the man or woman, but equally an office which seems to imply power reveals the person. In reality, a college or university administrator has only the power that his or her worth as a person and as an educational leader earns. Because of long tradition and an atmosphere of mutual respect in the community of scholars at its best, a position or office may be a vehicle of great influence—power in its best sense. That the genuine and proper power may be protected, care must be taken to distinguish carefully between the office and the person who occupies it—the office may be sacred, the occupant is a temporary tenant.

Confusing the office with the person may manifest itself in many ways, of course, but one of the most frequent and often subtly offensive is for the administrator to speak in the possessive of the institution where he or she serves and of its parts—for example, "my faculty," "my department chairman," in the manner of a general speaking of "my troops" or a king of "my subjects." In a college or university, the administrator, however exalted the office, is first among equals. It is best that the language used, as well as the action, recognize this fact.

Principle 36 Relations with the Lay Board

FOR THE ADMINISTRATOR EFFECTIVE RELATIONS WITH THE BOARD OF TRUSTEES OR REGENTS ARE CRUCIAL TO ALL ELSE, BUT MUST NOT BE BOUGHT AT TOO GREAT A PRICE.

In Higher Education in the United States, the System of Governance Is a Delicate Balance among the Administration, the Faculty and Staff, the Students, and the Lay Board of Trust. It Is of Utmost Importance That Each Part of This Balance Understand Its Role and Especially Its Limitations: Although Legal Power Is with the Lay Board, Actual Power in an Academic Community Is Very Diffused and Results from Mutual Respect and Confidence—Is Basically Not Legal or Categorical in Any Meaningful Sense.

The administrator, particularly the president, must have reasonably full confidence of the board of trustees of the institution. Since colonial days the lay governing boards have had a very significant influence in higher education in the United States. These boards have essentially the same position and responsibilities in all types of institutions of higher learning, ranging from the small hilltop liberal arts college to the complex modern publicly supported university. In general, the lay board of trust has the legal responsibility for the institution. They are thus responsible for its general policy to "the public" for whom the institution exists.

Nearly all of this power, especially as it applies to the educational processes of the institution, is delegated to the president (or more accurately, the president's office), which in turn delegates responsibility to the faculty, staff, and students as the nature and welfare of the institution require. The governance of the institution becomes, then, a delicate balance among these aspects of the community of scholars, especially the board, the administration, and the faculty.

The key to the success of this system lies chiefly in a deeply based, mutual respect and an intuitive understanding of the long-standing tradition that makes the system work. Although there are a few painful exceptions, the facts indicate that the system has worked remarkably well. This system of governance breaks down when any significant segment of the system seriously misconceives its role.

The faculty members, knowing that because of the nature of the higher learning they are, in essence, the institution, may become arrogant and fail or refuse to see the crucial role of the board, the administration, or the students. The president is always in danger of misinterpreting his or her very considerable power, forgetting that it exists only in a balance of mutual respect. The students, knowing that they are a central reason for the whole effort, deceived by the untried vision of youth, hurt by inept procedures, discouraged by unimaginative teaching, and disturbed by an unsettled society, may expect more influence in the governing process than their expertise and experience warrant. The board, aware of its legal power, may forget that legal power is nothing in an institution of higher learning unless it rests upon an understanding of the nature of higher education, confidence, and mutual respect. Evidently, a lay board is helpless to produce or maintain a community of scholars.

As mentioned earlier, it is remarkable that each of these groups has played its part so well in the history of American education. Yet it must be said that there may be a growing tendency for lay boards, especially those that are elected (principally community or junior college boards), to misconceive their proper role. When this happens it may result from neglect on the part of the chief administrator to make clear the essential nature of effective academic governance.

Evidently, the president is an extremely important factor in this delicately balanced system. It is of utmost importance that the chief administrative officer (first among many equals with highly specialized competencies) and educational leader must have the respect and confidence of all parts of the community of scholars. Especially, the administrator should have the confidence of the board of trustees. Presidents, then, are wise to make their positions on basic issues, including their approach to administrative problems, clear to the board at the time the person is being considered for the position of president. The temptation is strong, especially if one wants a position, for the candidate to try to guess what the board wants and to agree to follow those wants. This approach usually leads to trouble. A president is not like a fearful person, seeking favor and a position; he or she is more like a physician or attorney being asked to consider assuming a special responsibility warranted by training, experience, and qualities as a person.

At the same time, the president respects the board and understands its far-reaching responsibility as well as that of other parts of the institution. The point here is that the president should not be offered the position nor should it be accepted unless he or she has the respect and confidence of the board. How that respect can be retained involves all the principles discussed in this book. At what point an official should resign if mutual confidence begins to erode is a very complex matter which will be different for each specific case. In general, it can be said that a president should, for personal welfare and that of the institution, gracefully resign when it is clear over a reasonable period of time that the confidence of the board has been lost.

PART III

Theoretical Considerations: Background for Principles

INTRODUCTION

We present in this section of the book a few of our ideas about the nature and purpose of the higher learning, and the processes that are basic to the optimum administration of colleges and universities. These pieces have been used as a basis for presentation before various faculty groups and organizations. In some cases they have been previously published, but are not widely available.

They are presented here to provide some theoretical framework for the principles which are the essence of the book, and to stimulate discussion on the basic issues which underlie the sound administration of institutions of higher learning. These thoughts are not intended to be definitive, but are suggestions of a conversation that is endless and is the essence of the higher learning in process. There is some repetition, but we find that in this kind of book the repetition of basic points gives desired focus and emphasis and thus is a strength: Themes and even the same music are repeated often in a great symphony.

1. THE HIGHER LEARNING: TEACHING AND RESEARCH IN COLLEGE AND UNIVERSITY

The best brief statement on the nature and purpose of the higher learning that we have been able to formulate is the following:

> The essence of the higher learning is the search for truth and its relation to all of life; a search expressed through (a) the study of the experience and achievement of man, especially the best he has achieved, (b) the "imaginative consideration" of the implications of that achievement for the present and the future, and (c) the persistent study of all aspects of reality by direct observation. This interaction among students, teachers, and the records of man's experience goes on in an atmosphere characterized in some degree by freedom, adventure, imagination, endless inquiry, and Socratic humility.

The key aspect of the concept of the higher learning since Plato attempted first to put the idea into action in his Academy beginning about 387 B.C. is that the process must include in a dynamic relationship teaching and research—the imparting of that already known or discovered and the constant search for new knowledge either in the nature of theory or fact. In the higher learning, the spirit and act of inquiry must be central and pervasive.

The genius of the higher learning, and the concept is one of the five or six most important ideas discovered by humanity, is that it is a community of scholars—younger scholars who have achieved certain skills and maturity, usually called secondary education, and older

59

scholars who have achieved a high level of scholarship in a particular field or several fields, who have pursued the spirit of inquiry to make discoveries, and who continue the search. These younger and older seekers, for the best result, work in a physical community composed of buildings and grounds conducive to the higher learning process. There are libraries, laboratories, museums, playing fields, chapels, lawns, and works of art: whatever has been found to contribute to carrying on most effectively the teaching and discovery which are the essence of the process. This community of scholars is responsibly free under a system of self-government.

This level of education when done well serves two great purposes. It provides the higher, in a sense final, formal aspect of the education of the citizens of a democracy. Such citizens learn or understand at a beginning level the best the race has discovered and, at the same time, develop the spirit and skills of endless inquiry. For most of human history this process was reserved for the most gifted, who were thought to be able to profit from this effort and who thus became the leaders of the society. The United States, after the Civil War particularly, began to propose that all citizens, or nearly all, could profit from the higher learning, for in a self-governing society all citizens are assumed to have great potential, and to need advanced knowledge, understanding, and the spirit of continuous inquiry. Secondly, it extends the areas of knowledge and understanding—pushes back the frontiers of what is known and understood—through research, which includes all methods of search for new knowledge and insight. These methods, in general, include:

(a) objective observation characterized by measurement and epitomized by carefully designed experimentation, usually called the method of natural science; (b) careful thought about what has been observed and the problems faced—the method of reason or logic, philosophy at its best; (c) intuition—the poetic or prophetic vision in which especially gifted persons seem to perceive reality directly, as in various types of creative activity in the arts, and by special insights, as in religion.

In the best atmosphere of search these three methods work in cooperation and mutual respect, often closely interacting in any endeavor. However, the three methods frequently are in conflict and fail to cooperate or at times work in opposition. Then the search for new truth may become partial or fragmentary and consequently ineffective or harmful.

The higher learning at its best creatively interrelates its two great purposes, teaching and research, so that both have a special quality. Perhaps the ingredient that is most important and must be pervasive in the higher learning is the attitude and purpose of inquiry or investigation, a term President William Rainey Harper was fond of using. Thus research or creativity is given purpose, meaning, and responsibility because of its close relation to teaching; for what is discovered and the process of discovery are crucial to the educative endeavor. Equally important, all teaching in the higher learning is inspired and enlivened by the spirit and activity of inquiry. To separate the two either in attitude or practice is to seriously diminish both. So the great institutions of higher learning are always institutions of teaching and institutions of research. Herein lies their genuine greatness.

One final word: Although what has been argued in this paper holds throughout the higher learning, evidently the center of emphasis varies greatly from institution to institution and among types of institutions. The liberal arts college, the community college, the undergraduate college of the university, and the professional school likely will place the emphasis on the teaching and the professional training aspects; the research-oriented university, particularly the graduate school, and the special-purpose institutes place the central emphasis upon the research and the creative aspects. Of course, education at all levels involves both inquiry and teaching. But these facts in no way negate the basic principle that the higher learning is a special type of creative and dynamic combination of teaching and research, provided at a particular level of development. If this principle were better understood by all engaged in the higher learning, much tension centering in the relation between teaching and research could be reduced or overcome to the improvement and strengthening of both teaching and research and of the higher learning in general.

2. HIGHER EDUCATION IN MODERN SOCIETY

Higher education carries a heavy responsibility in modern society. No institution has greater opportunities to contribute significantly to the upward movement which modern man must achieve. Higher education at its best is the only institution in modern society that is free to seek answers to all the problems that confront humanity through the use of every method the mind can conceive. By its very nature the primary allegiance of higher education is to truth: its discovery, its wide dissemination, and its effective application to the questions of life. Thus, in theory, colleges and universities have no vested interests that would influence either ends or means. Their task is the full exploration of the nature of all phases of reality—a free, never-ending search that ranges from the nature of a grain of sand or a leaf to the nature of love or faith or Ultimate Reality.

This process involves essentially two things. Higher education passes on to the rising generations that which human beings have learned from their experience on this planet. This rich achievement has been deposited chiefly in the records of behavior, most clearly perhaps in books, but also in objects such as buildings, tools, and instruments. The results of experience are apparent also in organizations, institutions, and complex customs. It may be that the richest ore in the deposit of experience is living language. Indeed every language symbol is a concentrate of almost limitless experience. All of these records or deposits taken together are the culture of humanity.

Higher education proposes to give young men and women the benefit of that long and rich experience. Thus to transmit the culture is to enable the new generation to profit from all society has learned. The first responsibility is, in Ortega's phrase, to bring those educated "to the height of the times," which means to understand and live in terms of the best that people have learned. This transmission of the culture is not a passing on of dead knowledge, attitudes, and processes. As Professor Whitehead has so vividly pointed out, to be effective the transmission must be the "imaginative consideration of learning," essentially a creative uniting of the spontaneity of youth with the discipline and caution of age.

The second large task of higher education is search and discovery. Although human beings have had a long and profitable experience, very little has been learned about reality. As Newton said about his achievements, "I do not know what I may appear to the world; but to myself I seem to have been only like a boy playing on the seashore, and diverting myself in now and then finding a smoother pebble or a prettier shell than ordinary, whilst the great ocean of truth lay all undiscovered before me." The spirit of the higher learning is this free, unceasing search for new truth.

Throughout the process of transmission (described in the foregoing), the unfettered spirit of inquiry is central. Every previously established fact, every insight suggested by prophet, seer, poet, scientist, or magician is imaginatively and critically considered in the all-engaging spirit of search and research. Thus, by constantly throwing all previously known things into new combinations and by skillful probing through intuition or experimentation into the unknown, error is corrected and new truth is discovered.

Here then is a beginning conception of the nature and purpose of higher education: to assist people to learn the essence of what has been learned up to now, and to continue the search for additional truth, embedding in those who have the experience of the higher learning the humble but fearless spirit of endless inquiry. Of course, colleges and universities are not the only places where teaching and research go on, but these processes are the prime opportunity and responsibility of higher education. Whenever these things take place with zest and in freedom, there the spirit of the higher learning, the idea of the university, exists and does its incomparable work.

Throughout history, the experience of the higher learning has been limited to a very small proportion of the population. Professor

Arnold Toynbee suggests that this limitation was often deliberate in order to reserve the specific benefits for a particularly select group, often from a given social class, extended occasionally to the highly gifted of other classes. This ancient doctrine of the elite was usually rationalized by the argument that only those of very special ability and background could profit from higher education.

In a sense the argument was sound and indeed continues to be sound, for the higher learning experience was mediated through a vocabulary and special skills available to only a highly privileged group. Thus, a circular process became established that inevitably upheld the arguments which were used to support the limitation of educational opportunity: Only those of the privileged class had the opportunity to learn the skills and the attitudes of mind which enabled them to partake in the critical and imaginative consideration of the heritage of the race. All others (except a specially gifted and strongly motivated few) either had no opportunity or incentive to partake of the process or, when they attempted it, failed, and thus supported the primary argument on which the theory of limitation was based.

It is interesting and, in a sense, frightening to note that this situation continues to exist in nearly all nations of the modern world. We believe that this condition is the most fundamental obstacle to the development of a genuinely modern world civilization that might face and eventually solve some of man's most urgent problems.

The philosophy of severely limiting the higher education experience continued in full force in the United States until after the War Between the States, although a new spirit had been struggling toward birth in the work of Franklin, Jefferson, Eliphalet Nott, Wayland, Horace Mann and others. After 1865, there were great developments both in theory and practice which opened higher education to more and different people. The land-grant college movement, the work of White at Cornell, Angell at Michigan, Eliot at Harvard, the development of normal schools which grew into state colleges, the rapid growth of the "hilltop" church-related college, the evolution of the great Midwestern state universities, and especially the concept and growth of the junior college comprised a far-reaching and basically new approach to higher education.

The doctrine of the elite designed to limit educational opportunity at the college and university level was contrary to the essence of the American vision for mankind and society. This great experiment in democracy could not be given a fair trial until a new educational philosophy had come into being and had been put into practice. This meant that higher education must be made available to all the people who could profit from it, without regard for social and cultural background or special notions of ability. But the concept of the nature of higher education and who could profit from it had been thousands of years in growing. The limiting point of view and practices were embedded in custom, law, institutions, and even language. No departure that the American Republic undertook has required more profound changes in both thought and practice. It therefore should be no mystery that the goal of making higher education available to a wide variety of the population has really never been accepted as a sound philosophy nor put fully into practice.

Nevertheless, great strides have been made and the struggle still rages. Although remnants of the doctrine of the elite may yet be observed in considerable force everywhere in this society, not least within the ranks of higher education itself, a steadily increasing number and proportion of American young people want to go to college and actually do go. That is, the magnificent process of the higher learning is opened up to more and more people, most of whom, at any other time or place in the history of humanity, would not have had this opportunity.

The United States is determined to open up the experience of the higher learning (the transmission of the heritage and the urgent spirit of inquiry) to all of its people who can profit from the process. Further, higher learning is being studied carefully to find changes that might make it more profitable to those of high or special ability and of different levels and types of ability.

3. THE GOVERNANCE OF HIGHER EDUCATION: SOME BASIC PRINCIPLES

Background. An understanding of any significant problem requires that it be set in the context of the time. We must keep in mind two crucial aspects of our time. First, society in general. Apparently we are passing through a profound transitional period in the history and development of our species. Change always has been characteristic of the world, and probably of the wider universe. But in the history of the past there seem to have been a few—perhaps four or five—major transitional periods when man changed his major approaches to life. The evidence indicates that we are in the midst of one of the major transitional periods. During such times almost everything is unsettled; such times are very painful for individuals and for organized groups. Following these transitions we may go upward or downward: The risk is great and the opportunity is great.

We are too near our time of transition—sometimes called a time of trouble—to predict very well what may happen to us; yet we should like to share with you an intuitive, a poetic, feeling we have about our time. We believe that we are toward the end of an age, and that we are ready to move forward or upward again in our long tortuous climb. We fear that many of us, perhaps most of us, have been wounded or crippled or distracted by recent history and are unprepared to play a part in the great drama about to be staged which will involve reform and change in almost every aspect of life. This opportunity lies before us. If we are too small, petty, selfish, or shortsighted to play a role in the drama to be staged, others will appear who can do it, for the purposes of history—should we say the purposes of God?—cannot be thwarted.

66

Second, the place of higher education. Higher education is set in the midst—at the very core—of this society in transition. A little later we will discuss the nature and purpose of the higher learning in more detail, but suffice it to say that the higher learning has been developing in Western civilization since the founding of Plato's Academy in 387 B.C.; it has been the major means of educating the leadership for society and for discovering new truth—new knowledge—needed for the progress of society.

Throughout most of this period it has gained and kept the respect of the society, which meant that it had the degree of autonomy and freedom necessary to the doing of its great work. That freedom, respect, and support have been remarkable in the United States. There is in our time great danger of losing the confidence of the supporting community and thus the autonomy and freedom necessary to our work: Governance is at the very heart of this danger.

The nature, purpose, and process of higher education. In its present form the higher learning has been developing in Western civilization since about 1000 A.D., since the rise of the University of Paris, the universities in Italy, and, just a little later, the great universities of Oxford and Cambridge in England. This concept of the higher learning has produced similar institutions over the whole world. There is substantial literature on this development and, perhaps even more important, a great body of practice and tradition crucial to the essence of the higher learning.

It is of utmost importance that anyone or any group that has responsibility for the higher learning have some knowledge of and respect for this nature, purpose, and process. Indeed, perhaps the most ominous fact of our time is that many people, both inside (administration, faculty, staff, students) and outside (boards, legislators, alumni, concerned citizens) the community of scholars, are assuming power and responsibility about the higher learning without knowledge of and respect for its basic nature and purposes. A distinguished English educator expresses the thought in this way: "Do not meddle in the affairs of the university unless you know it well and love it well."

In essence, the higher learning is an organized, basically self-governing community of scholars, designed to search for and to teach the truth—the nature of things. In practice, this process involves two closely related tasks: (1) to transmit to the mature young—those who have completed secondary school—in a spirit of imaginative inquiry the best of knowledge, skill, and wisdom that our species has so far achieved; and (2) to push back the frontiers of knowledge, skill and wisdom through the continuous search for new truth, using essentially three approaches: intuitive and creative insight, logic or reason, and the scientific method. In doing these two tasks, the higher learning renders an incomparably important service to society.

The purpose of the governance of the higher learning. By now the logic of our thought becomes clear. The basic purpose of the governance of the higher learning is to create and protect the conditions for each community of scholars that will enable it to do its work effectively. Appropriate and adequate governance then means life and health for the higher learning; inappropriate and ill-conceived governance means frustration, conflict, confusion, and deterioration. That is how important the subject of governance is.

The current status of the governance of higher education. We must be honestly frank and face our situation squarely: Governance in higher education is in a dangerously bad state. Our method of governing our institutions of higher learning is, in the main, inappropriate and grossly inadequate to its task. The gravity of this fact becomes clear when we remember (1) the crucial significance of the work of the higher learning to the life of a society, and (2) the fact that the ability of the higher learning to do that work depends upon the nature and quality of its governance. When the higher education effort was small and concerned only with very special groups of highly selected faculty and students and was not dependent economically on the general community, which was the case until recent times, the academic community—the community of scholars—could be governed largely by tradition. Indeed, the spirit of the general academic community was such that it needed relatively little formal governance, except, perhaps, in the case of the perennial problems of student behavior. A modified model of the family sufficed rather well.

With greatly increased enrollments and corresponding increases in faculty, many of whom have little knowledge of, or respect for, the spirit of the higher learning, the paternal model does not work. The corporate model, patterned after business, which has tended to be in vogue in recent decades, is even less effective, for its hierarchy of authority threatens the very essence or meaning of the higher learning. The same is true, perhaps even more so, of a governance patterned after the ways of organized labor or the political state. (We regret that space does not allow us to say why, as we see it, none of these models will really do as a way to govern higher learning. Evidently, there are some aspects of all models of governance which are appropriate and useful for the higher learning.)

Let us generalize in this broad, not very satisfactory fashion: None of the ways of governance which we see in the society around us fits the needs of the community of scholars. Therefore, we are in desperate (the word is not too strong) need of a workable model for academic governance. Not having even a reasonably effective system, we flounder dangerously. Radical proposals all along the political spectrum flow into this vacuum. The problem is acute in all institutions and at all levels of education in California. So it is in Utah and in New York, Florida, Michigan—all over the nation. The problem is urgent at about the same level of intensity in all types and sizes of institutions. There is great danger that this problem unsolved will seriously damage the higher learning in the United States. In short, governance is crucial to all our vexing problems in higher education.

Toward a valid, viable method of governance for the higher learning. We are not ready or competent to propose a model of governance for higher education. (Surely we all wish that some of us could manifest the creative genius that our Constitutional Convention showed during that fateful summer of 1787 at Philadelphia. We fear we cannot expect that.) We seem to need more thought and study before that task is attempted. We propose, in the light of what we have already said, to suggest some principles that must be kept in mind as a sound system of governance is developed. Here is a brief tentative list:

1. The essence of the higher learning is a local group of scholars, which we call a college or a university, organized and maintained to achieve certain purposes. Such a community of scholars must be self-governed in such a way as to provide a maximum degree of freedom and variety with a maximum amount of order and responsibiity.

2. The employer-employee relationship is not appropriate for an academic community. A college or university is fundamentally dif-

ferent from business, military, and governmental organizations that so influence, indeed almost dominate, modern thought and behavior. The teacher-scholar (the faculty member) in an institution of higher learning is in reality an "officer" of the "corporation" and in no conventional sense an employee. The Faculty Members do not work for the college; they are the college. In a college or university the faculty are responsible members of a self-governing community whose relative autonomy is crucial to the nature and process of the higher learning.

3. In a democratic society such as ours, the larger supporting society, such as the political state or segment of it or an organized church, has a deep and legitimate concern about the conduct of the higher learning. Hence, lay boards representing that larger community have been given basic legal responsibility for our institutions of higher learning. The genius of this system is that these lay boards, which represent the public immediately and faithfully, delegate their educational authority and responsibility to the community of scholars (administration, faculty, and students). Very often these lay board members are alumni. The system works well only when this delicate balance and delegation are deeply embedded in the traditions and processes of the higher learning. The first requisite of an effective lay board in higher education is that it know and respect its limitations. The record of these boards has, in the main, been good.

4. In the governance of higher education all concerned with the higher learning should be represented and heard: the general public (represented by various levels of boards), the administration, the faculty, the patrons, the students, the staff, the alumni. The key principle is cooperation, and broad deep trust based upon a growing knowledge of the nature and importance of the higher learning in the society.

5. The faculty of a local campus (and the faculty includes the president, deans, department heads, etc., who are given certain special responsibilities) is the essence of the higher learning. Faculty members must have the central place in governance; they can have that place only if they earn it and hold it by virtue of what they are as scholar-teachers and as highly trained men and women of purpose, dedication, and integrity.

6. The colleges and universities must gain and hold the confidence

and basic respect of the larger supporting community (the political state or a segment of it, the church, or other group). The academic community should respect and continuously inform the supporting community. Most important, it must do its work well and with utmost responsibility. There is no responsibility comparable in importance to that of providing the best educational experience for the college and university students of a society.

7. Because of the basic nature and crucial importance of its unique work, it is of prime importance that the higher learning be kept out of politics as much as possible; that is, clear of the pressures and special pleadings of factions and particular interest groups. The higher learning is a very special process; those responsible for it should understand and, in essence, love it. This need to be free from the worst aspects of partisan politics is as important among faculty on campus as it is for boards and legislators. When the higher learning becomes a political pawn to be played with to achieve special ends not proper to its purposes, then the higher learning will be damaged. It should be remembered that well-selected lay boards and well-selected presidents are an excellent protection against dragging colleges and universities into the ugly struggle of partisan politics.

8. No system of governance is any better than the people who use it or who make it up. This principle is perhaps the most important of all. We must produce, and we must be, the kind of people who can govern the community of scholars in terms of the noble—we believe incomparable—purposes and processes of the higher learning. We should face the fact that we do not have such people in adequate supply. We know that at our institutions we often tend to be petty, shortsighted, self-seeking, and cynical. There is no magic system of governance that will overcome these shortcomings in people. We know that we are human and must expect to have human faults, but we believe that by deeply caring and by giving thought we could do much better than we usually do. Our greatest need is mature men and women who understand and believe in the higher learning. One of the goals of our institutions should be to produce more such people.

9. In order to protect and promote the legitimate and vital integrity of the local institution and to guard against harmful centralization, optimum use should be made of local lay boards for individual institutions. These boards can work within broad coordination poli-

cies. Without such boards with real responsibility and close meaningful relation with the local institution, the drift toward overcentralization is almost inevitable.

Some practical suggestions. We wish to offer a few common sense, practical suggestions that may be helpful. These suggestions are almost personal in nature, but they are based upon a lifetime of experience with a variety of institutions, a careful study of the literature of the higher learning, a long study of the literature on political government, and a study of the vast and varied writing on the nature and behavior of human beings:

1. Do not allow the academic community to be divided from the general supporting community. In a democracy we must have the support and confidence of the larger community, not only financial support but also moral support; that larger community must understand and believe in what we are doing. We should take care to avoid offending unnecessarily the Judeo-Christian ideals which are at the base of our civilization.

2. We should not allow ourselves to be foolishly divided on our various campuses and among our institutions. Of course, there should be freedom, variety of opinion, and much diversity, but also genuine concord on the factors crucial to the higher learning, and the courtesy and deep goodwill that respect for reason and evidence fosters. This confidence should contribute greatly to this variety within diversity.

3. We should take every possible opportunity to discuss the higher learning with all who are interested, but especially with the leaders in all segments of the society: political, cultural, religious. An active conversation or dialogue should be kept open; there should be more understanding of the issues crucial to the higher learning: research, teaching, tenure, freedom, etc. Our leaders, particularly our presidents, must constantly interpret the meaning of the higher learning to the people of a state.

4. The alumni should be brought into our affairs in every possible way. They were once a part of the community of scholars and, in a deep sense, they should remain so. They should understand and believe in what we are doing. Their interest, understanding, and support are indispensable to our general effectiveness.

5. The community of scholars must not be for sale nor give the appearance of being so. We need money, of course, but that money must come and will come because people believe in what we are doing.
6. We must take all diligence to keep our own houses in order. If we do not wisely discipline ourselves, then we will lose not only our precious and necessary freedom but also the support we need. This is a touchy matter, but we are confident that institutions have been hurt by allowing behavior that has nothing to do with genuine academic freedom and autonomy.

Now one final concluding statement:

The problems of the governance of the higher learning are complex and delicate. They arise out of and reflect the nature and purpose of the higher learning. The governance of higher education must provide almost complete freedom for the community of scholars and, at the same time, equally complete order. This balance must be achieved in such a way as to gain and hold the confidence of the supporting community. The task is difficult, but in no sense impossible. The key to its solution is in the quality of the people in the higher learning, particularly those in leadership responsibility. People who understand the higher learning and respect it can and will find an appropriate system of governance for this crucial organization in human life. People who are self-seeking, who lack an understanding of the essences of colleges and universities, will damage or destroy the higher learning in their attempt to govern it. Our situation is not unlike the one of which Lincoln spoke when he said: "The dogmas of the quiet past are inadequate for the stormy present. The occasion is piled high with difficulty and we must think anew and act anew. We must disenthrall ourselves, and then we shall save our country."

4. A NEGLECTED DIMENSION OF EDUCATIONAL LEADERSHIP: THE LEADER AS A PERSON

Introduction

Before we come to the major thoughts to be considered under this topic, a few introductory points will serve as a meaningful background for the major ideas. This quotation from Emerson will set the tone for these thoughts: "Blind men in Rome complained that the streets were dark. To the dull mind all nature is leaden. To the illuminated mind the whole world burns and sparkles with light."

The special tensions of our times make balanced thought and clear perspective difficult. We are all influenced by the series of emergencies that have faced us since the close of the Second World War: the prolonged Cold War; the Korean conflict, about which we were divided; the Vietnam war, which threatened to be endless and divided us even further; the constant possibility of worldwide atomic war, the horrors and consequences of which we could hardly face even in imaginative prospect; the peacetime draft, which did much to poison the higher learning; and all of this culminating in a sort of wild upheaval—like the bursting of a long festering boil—in the late Sixties and early Seventies, which seemed, for the moment at least, to threaten the very foundations of our civilization, especially the American Republic, which is the great experiment in civilization-building in our age. And then, as this storm subsided, the strange, deeply demoralizing situation in the national government developed and culminated in the first resignation of a U.S. President in our history. In the face of this situation, the nation had to deal with extremely complex and difficult problems. Such a series of emergencies tends to distort perspective and generate panic, demanding the very best of leadership qualities on our part.

A second background factor of importance for our thought is the fact that our state of California is an epitome of the rest of the country, and perhaps of the rest of the world. Whatever problems are acute in our rapidly developing society, appear first and in bold outline in California; but it is equally true that our opportunities are unmatched: In the words of an ancient proverb, the crises we face in California society, in general and in education particularly, present great dangers and great opportunities. Let us emphasize and be ready to use the opportunities.

As a final introductory word, we speak of education. We have a deep respect for public education in the United States and in California. It is almost self-evident that the effectiveness and future welfare of a self-governing people are dependent upon the quality of its education. Our accomplishments in education, although not all we would like them to be, are great: No people at any time in history or at any place on the globe has provided such widespread opportunity for schooling. Of course, there is reason to be concerned about the quality of that education and of the teachers and administrators who provide it. The thesis of this section is that there is a crucial dimension increasingly lacking in education that threatens to undermine its central quality and power. Here we cannot consider teachers nor curriculum, both of which interest us deeply; rather, our purpose is to think with those who are the administrative leaders of our schools. Our central concern is: What is the missing dimension in modern leadership, especially educational leadership?

Perhaps it will help us to think better together if we outline our approach:

A. The background of our present situation: Where are we and how did we get here?

B. An assessment of our situation: What are the major strengths and the major weaknesses that compose that situation?

C. The meaning and nature of the creative leadership we need: What are the central qualities of effective leadership?

D. The quality of the leader as a person as the key.

E. A few practical suggestions that may help.

Evidently these major points can only be briefly sketched in one brief section. The quality of the readers makes a detailed discussion unnecessary. They can fill in the argument.

A. Some background of the present situation. Our lives have been cast in a special time of trouble which may be the forerunner to, or indeed an early part of, one of the great transitional periods in the history of humanity. The latter part of the 19th century was a high point in human development: In the fifty years prior to 1914, Western people made remarkable progress toward building a good civilization. It seemed that we were on the way toward the elimination of some of the major evils that had so long cursed us: Children were better treated; labor conditions greatly improved; women began to achieve equality; medicine, agriculture, transportation, etc., as a result of advances in science, made great strides; and, perhaps most important of all, education became widely available. Many believed, and they had good reason, that humanity approached a great new era.

But instead, the First World War came in 1914, and that was the beginning of the prolonged time of turmoil and trouble in which our lives have been cast. We do not need to give the details of this period: the First World War followed by a demoralizing world-wide Depression, the Second World War with its incomparable destruction, the release of atomic energy used first in the bomb, the extended Cold War, and the upheaval of the Sixties and early Seventies. Of all this we are painfully aware. We have been in a continuous emergency for more than half a century: As a result, we have become emergency minded, often dealing irrationally and even frantically with what ordinarily would be small problems.

This sad tale is sketched here not to emphasize the negative or to gloat over our troubles—there has been too much of that in our time—but as preparation for the assessment of the present time: There is reason to believe we may have come to the end of an age and the beginning of a new one, for which the trouble and tragedy just described were a preparation—perhaps a necessary preparation. In the early Seventies we may have reached a very special point in history. We may be turning a sort of psychological and spiritual corner—moving out of a period of strange and prolonged confusion and darkness, and entering into a new period when humanity will go forward again. If this vision is true, we will need new people for this new world which is yearning to be born—most especially we will need new leaders at all levels of society: men and women who are not too badly distorted by the fears and prejudices of the confused and troubled past.

Many of us may have been seriously wounded or even diseased by our struggle with the past. Many of us have become cynical and embittered, unable to believe in ourselves, in humanity, in God, in the future. If we are not ready for the world that longs to be born—that *will* be born—if we are unequal to its demands, other men and women will appear. We need people of faith who can believe, people of hope who can give themselves totally to the tasks at hand, people of love whose ends and means are in proper relation, and people of integrity whose ideals and actions form a unity, a whole. We do not mean perfect people—that is not possible—but ordinary people who have a renewed vision of what life should and can be and are working together toward that vision.

We deeply know that nothing less will do for the future that must come. That is the vision: What can we do about it?

B. The strengths and weaknesses of our present situation: a frank look at the positive and negative aspects of where we are. What is the capital with which we can work; what are the major obstacles?

1. Space will allow us to mention only three great strengths:

(a) We have the resources of the technological advances of the past three hundred years or so. It is in vogue now to abuse and downgrade technology. The truth is that science and technology have done great things for humanity. The evils are not in science and technology, but in the foolish and irresponsible use we make of them.

(b) We have a remarkable system of government which reasonably well used can provide the justice, equal opportunity, freedom, and order necessary to a good life for humanity. We have not yet produced the citizens needed to make the system work at its best, but we will, and in the meantime the system has served us well these two hundred years. As a part of this strength, we must remember that this system rests squarely upon the great Judeo-Christian heritage, of the proper behavior of human beings and of the nature of Ultimate Reality or God. Without this foundation, the system, as great as it is, cannot work. Still this body of truth is widely known and respected—even if not widely practiced among us.

(c) This third strength is especially important for the subject under consideration. We have a huge, complex, and—all things considered—a remarkably effective system of schools. The access to education is magnificent; the support, in the main, excellent; the purpose noble. This far flung system of education is a resource of first magnitude. As is the case with technology, our task is to make maximum use of it.

The reader can add other strengths, and they are many indeed.

2. But what of the weaknesses—the liabilities? We must take a square look at the weaknesses, even though what we see is painful, for only then can we deal with them constructively.

(a) We suffer from a great loss of *faith*—a fatal loss in the ability *to believe* is a crucial weakness of our time. We do not refer only to loss of religious belief, but to a pervasive skepticism or cynicism that threatens the very meaning of life. This is the problem of values: what we consider true and important and why.

(b) A second great weakness of our time seems to be a consequence of the first: Apparently as a result of our failure in belief, there is a widespread deterioration of human character. The manifestations are numerous and often dramatic, as in violence, but what might be called simple manifestations are more seriously symptomatic. We refer to theft and lying. These two activities, widespread in a society, threaten its whole fabric. No resources amount to much without the will—the character—to use them wisely. This weakness threatens all that is good in our lives: We become like a child with a great treasure in his or her hands, or an imbecile with great power. Human character is the key problem of any time.

(c) Most serious of all our weaknesses or shortcomings is a scarcity of effective leadership at all levels of life and all phases of endeavor: The inevitable result of inadequate leadership is a general loss of confidence and of nerve. In such cases, the problems common to human life become insurmountable.

We come here close to the heart of our concern, so let us pause and summarize this point.

There is a dangerous circular effect or process produced by these three weaknesses. The loss of faith destroys the conditions necessary to the formation of strong and sound character; lack of character produces a soil which makes the rise of effective leadership difficult or impossible; without leadership there can be no effective endeavor at any level. Here then is where we are: The resources for a great forward movement for humanity are abundant and at hand; basically we know where we want to go and how to get there (the Judeo-Christian knowledge and vision have provided the goals and the means to them); as yet we are unable to make the journey. We are in danger of being on center, of being becalmed when the need for movement is great, almost desperate. The real task of our time is to break this circle so that the forward movement can take place. We believe it can be done—that it will be done in an encouraging degree in the years that lie immediately before us.

The center of our message—really a frightening message—is that this dangerous, destructive, vicious cycle can and must be broken at the point of leadership—especially of educational leadership—not by technical effectiveness as important as that is, but by the quality of the leader as a person: When that quality is lacking, all else fails, falls through.

C. What then is the nature and meaning of the creative leadership we must have to break the downward cycle and move forward again?

1. The leader epitomizes or represents what those who give him or her special responsibility consciously and unconsciously want: He or she must have a clear and vivid vision of what should be and can be. This vision must live or seem to live in the leader.

2. The leader must be able to express those sensed or felt needs in ways that can be understood. He or she must put into words and manifest in action and feeling what *should be.*

3. The leader must help those he or she leads to move toward the desired goals. Leadership is, in this sense, absolutely dependent upon success. He or she must have the courage and energy to persist in the realization of the vision of what should be—the leader believes in the goals and in the people who are a part of the endeavor in question.

D. The leader as a person. Now we come to the crucial or unique part of our thought. Boldly stated the point is simple though profoundly significant: The educational leader can be no greater as a leader than he or she is or is becoming as a person. In short, the leader must above all be a man or woman of genuine integrity and strong character. Here then is the prime need of our time.

It is not that persons who are in educational leadership must be superhuman or saints. They will be none of these, but to fill the need which we are emphasizing, they must be going in the right direction. If the leader as a person would have the power we seek, he or she must be growing in three great areas of life:

1. He or she must be growing in the area of knowledge: of self, of humanity in general, of his or her field of work, of history (what has been). Wide reading is a major source of this growth.

2. The educational leader must be growing in skill: the ability to apply what one knows with style to day-to-day work in order to constantly learn and improve. Such growth in skill is essential to the confidence necessary to a great leader.

3. The leader must be growing in *being*: in what one *is* in body, mind and soul. This area of growth is the special area of emphasis in this section, for it is in quality of spirit that we principally fall short in our time. What we are speaks so loudly that what we say cannot be heard; and if our being is empty, or stale or petty, even what we *do* or seem to do loses its power.

Some of the essences of being are these: faith, the ability to believe; vision, the ability to see that which should be and can be; courage, the strength to persist until one's vision becomes reality; humility, the capacity to expect and accept weaknesses and mistakes in ourselves and others; love or compassion, the growing capacity to forget oneself in the genuine service of a larger cause; peace, a feeling of oneness with the deeper forces of the universe.

Without this dimension of *being*, all knowledge and all skill eventually come to nothing. In the long run, only leaders who are growing in *being* can gain and retain the confidence we need to catch our balance and move forward again.

E. A few practical suggestions. We know from long personal experience, including a very uneven journey of growth, that the road we suggest is a steep and often rough one. We cannot conclude this section without offering a few practical suggestions that may be helpful to educators in this way of growth:

1. Learn to withdraw regularly for physical, mental, and spiritual renewal. A great enemy—perhaps the greatest enemy—of the quality of growth and of life we seek is fatigue, staleness, and the lowered energy of ill health. Often our former students now carrying the heavy load of administration respond that they do not have time for renewal. But time is always a matter of wise priorities. Let us never neglect the great good place of renewal.

2. Examine constantly your goals. The life of meaning arises from clear, large aims. Large goals firmly based in universals beyond oneself make large men and women; small, immediate aims narrowly based and closely related to self make small, petty, fearful persons.

3. Find and carefully cultivate a few friends of like mind and heart with whom you can walk the way of learning and growth. Among these should be at least one acute, friendly critic; someone who has the wisdom and the courage to warn us as we are about to enter one of those places that should be labeled "Wrong Way: Do not Enter." A leader is in constant danger of being isolated and hearing only what he or she wants to hear. We all need a loyal opposition close at hand.

4. Cultivate the deep roots of growth in being: meditation, wide reading, experience with great music and art and with nature.

5. Find a way of worship (which simply means a way of spiritual renewal) that is appropriate to your temperament. Such worship, whether formal or informal, seems to be the necessary nutrient for our deepest selves. Probably a great portion of modern men and women is spirit-starved and hence damaged in soul. Perhaps each of us in his or her special way can learn to worship, especially those of us who carry heavy responsibility and need so much to unite with power and wisdom beyond ourselves.

We close this section with a beautiful Sioux Indian prayer, which expresses well the deep spirit of worship of which we speak:

> Grandfather, Great Spirit, you have been
> always, and before you nothing has been.
> There is no one to pray to but you. The
> star nations all over the heavens are
> yours, and yours are the grasses of the
> earth. You are older than all need, older
> than all pain and prayer.

Grandfather, Great Spirit, all over the
world the faces of living ones are alike.
With tenderness they have come up out of
the ground. Look upon your children,
with children in their arms, that they
may face the winds and walk the good road
to the day of quiet.

Grandfather, Great Spirit, fill us with the
light. Give us the strength to understand
and the eyes to see. Teach us to walk the
soft earth as relatives to all that live.
Help us, for without you we are nothing.

5. ACADEMIC GOVERNANCE: SOME MISUNDERSTANDINGS

Extended paticipation in academic governance usually leads to two observations. Many of the participants are confused about their roles; and many of the participants nourish the expectation that there is, somewhere, a model system of government that will eliminate most of the problems that are common to the familiar systems. The first confusion reflects misconceptions of advisement and authority. The second may reveal the impossibility of separating personalities from process and a system.

Misunderstandings related to authority for decision-making and participation in decision-making seem especially prevalent among faculty representatives. The confusion is fostered by the common American style of control of higher education, which places the authority, both for public and independent institutions, outside the campus, in the hands of lay boards. Thus, while the faculty members dominate curricular and instructional decisions, the ultimate responsibility and authority for their performance rests in corporate or public hands.

In a manner that may add confusion, newer management techniques have emphasized participatory decision-making. Higher education, like business and industry, has seen in the past half-century a steady decline in authoritative management style. Corporate and college presidents rarely can or do "fire" someone in the earlier, uninhibited way.

The faculty senate may be the greatest single source of confusion concerning decision-making. It is typically a recommending body, one without authority; nevertheless its recommendations ordinarily appear to have authority, since the recommendations seem to result in subsequent positive responses from the president and the board. In a scaled-down manner, recommendations of various other academic bodies bring about decisions that reflect the recommendations of faculty or students. However, the decision-making authority remains with the board, emerging most clearly from time to time when the president refuses or contradicts a recommendation from faculty or students.

While there must be some campuses where the president and the faculty are content with the system for governance, the majority of systems reflect tensions which normally accompany the reconciliation of the conflicting needs of campus constituencies. Presidents commonly mention the time and energy consumed by obtaining a consensus from faculty and from students. Students frequently voice their frustration at faculty members' not posting or meeting their office hour commitments. Faculty members find themselves in conflict between meeting advisement responsibilities and the pressures for research and publication. Trustees feel a mandate to balance the budget; students want lower tuition; faculty members want a salary increase.

Not surprisingly, each of the constituencies may feel that a new system of governance might increase the likelihood of better conflict resolution, especially if the new proportions of representation benefit their constituency. However, since any increase in proportion must be accompanied by another's decrease, there is understandable resistance to substantive change that threatens to decrease any constituent's ability to participate in the decision process.

Many campus governance systems resemble one another, ranging from exclusive, single-constituent bodies, such as faculty senates, to multi-constituent bodies, including not only administration and students but community and staff representatives as well.

If success is defined as the ability of a system to function reasonably well in meeting the needs of its constituents and the ability to reach a consensus within a reasonable time, most kinds of systems can be successful. On the other hand, given personalities or constituencies which are intransigent or hostile, most kinds of systems can be unsuccessful.

When we examine those systems that seem to work reasonably well, we are likely to discover common characteristics which reflect effective relationships between personalities, constituencies, and the process of decision-making, almost regardless of the kind of system. For example, most of the key participants may see their system as imperfect, but not in need of replacement.

Clear, unimpeded communication is a characteristic of an effective system. Each constituency has at least one articulate spokesperson; equally important, each has several members who are capable and active listeners.

There is also evident what labor negotiators would call a high level of "maturity." The closest academic synonym seems to be empathy, the ability to perceive someone else's needs and problems. Reaching a consensus requires compromise; compromise is made easier by recognizing that others have needs; the most effective compromise is based on mutual empathy.

Patience seems to be another characteristic of participants in a successful academic decision-making system. This is not to recommend an unending passivity or docility. Patience can be abused and should be protected. However, those experienced with academic process recognize that immediate, simple responses are usually difficult to obtain. Faculty, students, and administrators have many competing demands and numerous constraints on their responses. On the other hand, they can be tardy without cause; consequently, patience must be tempered with persistence.

All of the campus constituencies gain from enhanced decision-making. Trustees depend on recommendations for their own policy decisions. The quality and timeliness of those recommendations should be enhanced by the system which enables the constituencies to formulate recommendations. However, when the process of arriving at recommendations seems ineffective, replacing or drastically revising the system may treat the symptoms rather than the cause of the problem.

Part IV

SELECTED REFERENCES

Note: This bibliography is very limited and selected, composed of general references that have been especially helpful to the authors and their advanced students. There is a very large bibliography available, particularly in general administration.

Atkinson, Brooks. *College in a Yard.* Harvard University Press, 1957.

Baldridge, J. Victor and others. *Policy Making and Effective Leadership.* Jossey-Bass, 1978.

Ben-David, Joseph. *American Higher Education: Directions Old and New.* McGraw-Hill, 1972.

Bok, Derek. *Beyond the Ivory Tower: Social Responsibilities of the Modern University.* Harvard University Press, 1982.

Bowen, Catherine Drinker. *Miracle at Philadelphia: The Story of the Constitutional Convention, May to September, 1787.* Little, Brown, 1966.

Boyer, Ernest L. and Hechinger, Fred. *Higher Learning in the Nation's Service.* The Carnegie Foundation for the Advancement of Teaching, 1981.

Brubacher, John S., and Rudy, Willis. *Higher Education in Transition.* Harper, 1976.

The Carnegie Foundation for the Advancement of Teaching. *The Control of the Campus: A Report on the Governance of Higher Education.* The Carnegie Foundation for the Advancement of Teaching, 1982.

Cordasco, F. *Daniel Coit Gilman and the Protean Ph.D.* E.J. Brill, 1960.

Corson, John J. *Governance of Colleges and Universities.* McGraw-Hill, 1960.

De Tocqueville, Alexis. *Democracy in America.* (Specially edited and abridged by Richard D. Heffner.) A Mentor Book, 1956.

Deutsch, Monroe E. (ed.). *The Abundant Life: Benjamin Ide Wheeler.* University of California Press, 1926.

Eddy, Edward D., Jr. *Colleges for Our Land and Time.* Harper, 1957.

Gardner, John W. *Self-Renewal.* Harper, 1964.

Geiger, Louis G. *Higher Education in a Maturing Democracy.* University of Nebraska Press, 1963.

Goheen, Robert F. *The Human Nature of a University.* Princeton University Press, 1969.

Graubard, Stephen R. (ed.). *American Higher Education: Toward an Uncertain Future.* Daedalus, Vol. I, Fall 1974; Vol. II, Winter 1975.

Harvard Committee. *General Education in a Free Society.* Harvard University Press, 1945.

Haskins, Charles H. *The Rise of Universities.* Cornell University Press, 1957.

Hawkins, H. *Between Harvard and America: The Educational Leadership of Charles W. Eliot.* Oxford University Press, 1972.

Hocking. W.E. *The Coming World Civilization.* Harper, 1956.

Hofstadter, Richard, and Hardy, C. DeWitt. *The Development and Scope of Higher Education in the United States.* Columbia University Press, 1952.

Hofstadter, Richard, and Metzger, Walter R. *The Development of Academic Freedom in the United States.* Columbia University Press, 1955.

Hofstadter, Richard, and Smith, Wilson. *American Higher Education: A Documentary History.* 2 Vol. University of Chicago Press, 1961.

Hutchins, Robert M. *The Higher Learning in America.* Yale University Press, 1937.

Jaeger, Werner. *Paideia: The Ideals of Greek Culture.* Vols. I, II and III. Oxford University Press, 1939.

Jaspers, Karl. *The Idea of the University.* Beacon Press, 1959.

Jeneks, Christopher, and Riesman, David. *The Academic Revolution.* Doubleday, 1968.

Kelley, Win, and Wilbur, Leslie. *Teaching in the Community Junior College.* Appleton-Century-Crofts, 1969.

Kerr, Clark. *The Uses of the University.* Harvard University Press, 1974.

MacIver, Robert M. *Academic Freedom in Our Time.* Columbia University Press, 1955.

McGregor, Douglas. *The Human Side of Enterprise.* McGraw-Hill, 1960.

Millett, John D. *The Academic Community: An Essay on Organization.* McGraw-Hill, 1962.

Morison, Samuel E. *Three Centuries of Harvard.* Harvard University Press, 1937.

Murphy, William M., and Bruckner, D.J.R. *The Idea of the University of Chicago.* The University of Chicago Press, 1976. (Selections from the papers of the first eight chief executives of the University of Chicago from 1891 to 1975.)

Nevins, Allan. *The State Universities and Democracy.* University of Illinois Press, 1962.

Newman, J.H. Cardinal. *The Idea of a University.* Longmans, Green, 1947. (Originally published in 1856.)

Nisbett, Robert. *The Degradation of the Academic Dogma: The University in America, 1945-1970.* Basic Books, 1971.

Ortega y Gasset, Jose. *Mission of the University.* Routledge & Kegan Paul, Ltd., 1946.

Ortega y Gasset, Jose. *The Revolt of the Masses.* Norton, 1932.

Otten, C. Michael. *University Authority and the Student: The Berkeley Experience.* University of California Press, 1970.

Pettitt, George A. *Twenty-eight Years in the Life of a University President.* University of California Press, 1966.

Prator, Ralph. *The College President.* Center for Applied Research in Education, 1963.

Pullias, Earl V. *A Common Sense Philosophy for Modern Man: A Search for Fundamentals.* Philosophical Library, 1975.

Pullias, Earl V., and Young, James D. *A Teacher Is Many Things.* Indiana University Press, 1968; new edition 1977.

Pusey, Nathan. *The Age of the Scholar.* Harvard University Press, 1963.

Rudolph, Frederick. *The American College and University.* Knopf, 1962.

Sanford, Nevitt (ed.). *The American College.* John Wiley & Son, 1962. (Condensed and published as *College and Character,* 1964).

Schlesinger, Arthur M., Jr. and White, Morton. *Paths of American Thought.* Houghton Mifflin, 1963. (Especially Prologue, Epilogue, and Chapter I.)

Snow, C.P. *The Two Cultures and the Scientific Revolution.* Cambridge University Press, 1960.

Stone, James C., and DeNevi, Donald P. (eds.). *Portraits of The American University 1890-1910.* Jossey-Bass, 1971.

Storr, Richard J. *The Beginnings of the Future: A Historical Approach to Graduate Education in the Arts and Sciences.* McGraw-Hill, 1973.

Storr, Richard J. *Harper's University: The Beginnings.* University of Chicago Press, 1966.

Toynbee, Arnold. *A Study of History.* Oxford University Press, 1947 (abridgment of Vol. I-VI by D.C. Somerville).

Veysey, Laurence R. *The Emergence of the American University.* University of Chicago Press, 1965.

Weaver, David A. (ed.). *Builders of American Universities.* Shurtleff College Press, Vols. I, 1950; II, 1952; and III, 1969.

Whitehead, A.N. *The Aims of Education.* Macmillan, 1929.

Whitehead, A.N. *Adventures of Ideas.* Macmillan, 1933.

Whitehead, A.N. *Science and the Modern World.* Macmillan, 1925.

PART V

A NOTE ON THE TRAINING AND EXPERIENCE OF THE AUTHORS

Some knowledge of the authors may make the content and philosophy of this book more meaningful. Professor Pullias completed his elementary and secondary education in the public schools of Tennessee, did his college work at two small church-related liberal arts colleges in that state—two years at David Lipscomb College in Nashville, and two years at Cumberland University, Lebanon, Tennessee—where he received his B.A. in English. He taught English two years in a junior high school, and then went to the University of Chicago for the M.A. in the great School of Education there. Then he studied at the newly established Duke University on a graduate fellowship where he received the Ph.D. with a major in educational psychology and strong minors in education and in psychology. At this time, he developed a deep theoretical and research interest in the nature and development of personality, with special emphasis on mental health and the relationship of teaching and learning to personality.

As a graduate student and instructor at Duke, Professor Pullias began a career of college and university teaching which extended over about fifty years, and covered a variety of institutions of higher learning. In 1937, he accepted an invitation to join the faculty of Pepperdine College, then being established as a liberal arts church-related college in Los Angeles, to teach psychology and to develop a department in that area. He was granted a post-doctoral study leave and spent the year 1937-8 in special study in England, centering his work at the then-famous Tavistock Clinic in London, but studying with various distinguished persons in abnormal psychology and related fields. He returned to Los Angeles in 1938 to teach psychology. In 1940 he was invited to become Dean of the Faculty at Pepperdine College, where he served for seventeen years, at the same time continuing to teach psychology. Beginning in 1940 he began teaching courses in the summer session at the University of Southern California. In 1957, he was invited to U.S.C. to develop a doctoral program in higher education. This program engaged his efforts from 1957 to 1977, at which time he became Professor Emeritus. From 1940, he worked closely with the Western College Association, which became the Western Association of Schools and Colleges, the official accrediting agency of California and Hawaii, taking a special interest in newly estalished and developing institutions. He was chairman for two terms of the Commission on Higher Education of the California Teachers Association. As Professor of Higher Education at U.S.C. he taught advanced courses, directed the research of doctoral students, and did his own research and writing.

In 1954, Professor Pullias was appointed to the Los Angeles County Board of Education, and has served consecutively on that board to the present, completing thirty years of service on July 1, 1984. The Los Angeles County Superintendent of Schools Office has become one of the most respected and influential educational organizations in the state, and in many areas has attracted national attention. The Los Angeles County Board is the policy-making body for the Superintendent of Schools Office and, as such, has close knowledge of and relation to the California State Department of Education and the State Legislature, and very special relations with the ninety-five local school districts, including the Community College Districts, in Los Angeles County. This experience has given the senior author an intimate knowledge of public school administration.

In summary, the point of this brief account of training and experience is that all of his experience was a preparation for the writing of this book: The formal study of psychology and education, the teaching, the research and writing about higher education helped to form the ideas about the basic nature and processes of the higher learning and to suggest principles that are important to the effective administration of the academic community. Of course, the principles must stand on their own merit, must establish their own validity by their nearness to reality and by the clarity and aptness of their expression, but a little knowledge of their source and background may strengthen them.

Professor Wilbur was invited in 1965 to come in as the second full-time member of the developing Department of Higher Education at U.S.C., which now is the Department of Higher and Post-Secondary Education, to properly include the significant and growing aspect of continuing and adult education. At the time of Professor Wilbur's appointment, a wide search was made for the very best person to assist in the development of a first-rate Department of Higher Education. Professor Wilbur was selected to come in as an Associate Professor from a term as successful president of a developing community college in California. After about five years at the University, he was promoted to full Professor, and for the past nine years has served as Chairman of the department.

The department has developed rapidly, becoming one of the largest departments in the U.S.C. School of Education, and now has five full-time, tenure-track members, and a large number of adjunct and part-time persons who enrich certain special areas. The first doctorate with a major in Higher Education was awarded in 1961. As of September 1983, approximately 400 individuals had received doctorates with majors in this area. A large number of these students are in college and university administration in various capacities, upward of ten now serving as presidents of their institutions. Professor Wilbur has had a major part in training these men and women and remains in close contact with them in their work in the field.

Professor Wilbur, a native of California, attended the public schools in this state. He completed the first two years of college at Modesto Junior College (now Community College). After three years' service in World War II, he entered the University of Illinois at Urbana to earn his B.A. degree with a major in English and a special emphasis in Literature, which has remained a life-time interest. He also had a special summer at the Sorbonne for study of French Language and Culture. He received his M.A. in English at the University of California at Berkeley in 1951. Interested in teaching, he secured a position as teacher of English at Bakersfield Community College, where he taught for twelve years, serving the last two years as Assistant Dean. It was from his teaching position at Bakersfield and his part in the faculty there that he was invited to the Presidency of Barstow Community College.

In the meantime, Professor Wilbur had begun his work on his doctorate with a major in the area of Social and Philosophical Foundations. He received his Ph.D. in that area from U.S.C. in 1962. His major professor in philosophy, Professor Robert Brackenbury, who had received his own doctorate in educational philosophy from the University of Chicago, highly recommended Professor Wilbur for the appointment to the position in the Department of Higher Education at U.S.C., believing that his philosophic and sociological training and interest would strengthen the Department. Since coming to the Department of Higher Education, Professor Wilbur has taught advanced courses in this field with a special emphasis in college and university administration in the community college, directed doctoral research, and carried on his own research and writing. Among other things, he coauthored a significant book on the community college. He was appointed to the Commission on Higher Education of the influential California Teachers Association and served as its chairman one term. Also, Professor Wilbur has, since 1969, worked as a special consultant in the area of the community college in the Los Angeles County Schools Office. In this capacity, he has been a significant influence in the development of a consortium of community colleges that has created a program in educational television which has attracted national attention for its quality and promise.

Further, Professor Wilbur has been very active in the U.S.C. academic community with special emphasis in governance. He served one term as President of the All-University Senate at a very crucial time in the development of that influential body. In this position, he worked closely with the major administration of the University and with the Board, as well as with the faculty and student body. He has been selected to represent his colleagues on the chief committees and councils that govern the School of Education and the University as a whole.

Again, in this case, this background sketch of the training and experience of one of the authors of this book gives some notion of the view from which these ideas came. No account of a professional person's background can give a full picture, but perhaps that is not needed.

It should be added that Professor Pullias and Professor Wilbur have known each other for more than twenty years. Since 1965 they have worked intimately together in building the Department of Higher Education at U.S.C.

INDEX

academic freedom, 24, 26, 67
advice 13, 49, 83, 84
Angell, James B. 64
American Association of Universities 26
approval 21, 22, 23
atomic bomb 74, 76
atmosphere 6, 7, 25, 61
attitudes 18, 32
authority 13, 83, 84
autonomy 23, 67, 69, 70

balance 26, 27, 28, 37, 38, 44, 45, 48, 51, 52, 53, 73, 79, 80, 85
Bay of Pigs 37
being 80
Bowen, Catherine Drinker 48

Cather, Willa 43
centralization 71, 72
change 12, 28, 38, 65, 66
character 78, 79, 80
Civil War 60, 64
Cold War 74, 76

collective bargaining 24
Colonial college 29
communication 14, 20, 48, 85
compromise 85
confidence 15, 22, 38, 49, 51, 52, 53, 67, 70, 78, 80
confidentiality 35, 36, 49
conformity 31, 32
Constitutional Convention 48, 69
cooperation 4, 5, 70
courage 79, 80

delegation 52
democracy 60, 64, 65, 70, 75, 77
depression 76
dialogue 4, 57, 72
discipline 73
discussion 4, 57, 72
doctrine of the elite 64, 65
drift 12, 43
due process 18, 46
dynamics 12, 28, 38, 65, 66

ego 17

Eliot, Charles W. 18, 38, 64
emergency situations 18, 19
Emerson, Ralph W. 41, 74
emotionalism 41, 42
equity 21, 22

faith 77, 78, 79, 80
fragmentation 11, 12, 33, 84
Franklin, Benjamin 64
freedom (personal) 35
frustration 15

goals 46, 47, 79, 81
God 66, 77
governance 51-53, 67-71, 83, 84
growth 16, 27, 47, 80, 81

Harper, William Rainey 12, 61
Hitler, Adolph 41
humanness 16, 28, 71
humility 50, 51, 80

impatience 30
innovation 26, 27
inquiry 59, 60, 61
intuition 60, 63, 66
isolation 14, 29, 45, 49, 50

Jefferson, Thomas 48, 64
Judeo-Christian heritage 72, 77, 79

Kennedy, John F. 37
Korean Conflict 74

leadership 25, 71, 73, 78, 79
League of Nations 36

learning community 6, 43, 46, 52, 59, 60
learning environment 6, 7, 25, 61
Lincoln, Abraham 73
listening 19, 20, 28, 48, 49, 85
Lodge, Henry C. 35
love 77, 80
loyalty 33

Mann, Horace 64
Mann, Thomas 42
maturity 25, 71, 85
mistakes 17, 50
modern society 11, 25, 62, 64, 65, 66, 67, 74, 76, 77
morale 13, 14, 15, 17, 22, 34, 46, 74

Newton, Isaac 63
nineteenth century 29, 76
non-conformity 31, 32
Nott, Eliphalet 64

Ortega, Jose 63
Otten, C. Michael 31
overhead 34

parents 28
patience 85
peace 80
perfection 5, 77
personality of school 39, 40
personhood 79, 80
phoniness 21
Plato 24, 59, 67
planning 39, 42
politics 71

power 13, 18, 37, 50, 51, 52
practice 4, 5
prejudice 30
pressure 46
priorities 32, 33
progress 67
protection 25, 26
psychotics 19
purpose
  of book 3, 4, 5, 57
  of college or univ. 31, 59, 60,
    61, 63, 67

recreation 45, 80, 81
renewal 27, 80, 81
reprimanding 18
research 5, 63
respect 15, 20, 24, 30, 51, 52, 67,
  71
responsibility 13, 15, 30, 31, 37,
  39, 51, 52, 53, 62, 71
risks (risk-taking) 16, 18, 31, 45,
  46, 50
roles 13, 23, 24, 52, 53, 83

self-restraint 25, 35, 36
self-understanding 45
sensitive areas 17, 77
sensitivity 18, 21, 27, 28
"seventies" 26, 74, 76
silence 20, 48, 49

sincerity 21
"sixties" 26, 41, 74, 76
Sophocles 50
spirituality 80, 81, 82
stability 27, 52, 68
success 84, 85
support 49, 67, 72, 73, 81

teaching 5, 62, 63
technology 76, 77
tension 44, 45, 74, 84
tenure 24, 25
"the higher learning" 67, 68
thought 4
timing 27, 38, 44, 45
Toynbee, Arnold 64
tradition 27, 52, 68

Vietnam War 50, 74
vision 80

Washington, George 48
Wayland, Francis 64
Wheeler, Benjamin Ide 31
White, Andrew Dickson 64
Whitehead, Alfred N. 29, 63
wholeness 60
Wilson, Woodrow 36
wisdom 24, 42, 43
World War I 76
World War II 26, 76